The Incoherent Ramblings of an American Madman

JOEL SCOTT WATERMAN
| NEW YORK |

Contact: http://joelscottwaterman.weebly.com

Published by:

FriesenPress

Suite 300 – 852 Fort Street
Victoria, BC, Canada V8W 1H8

www.friesenpress.com

Distributed to the trade by The Ingram Book Company

TABLE OF CONTENTS

To Sandi,

Enjoy the ride!!.

" *May my thoughts*
flow freely until
I am empty "

With Respect,

Spartacus

About the Author

Joel Scott Waterman was born in Syracuse New York in 1963. He has lived and worked all over the United States and Canada, working on some of the largest construction projects in the world. He has also traveled throughout Europe and Mexico. Currently he resides in rural Upstate New York on the banks of the Ontiahantague'. He is a seasoned member of the biker world. Although an independent biker, he has lifelong friends in all segments of the motorcycle club community, from the 1% to 99%, nationwide. He has been in company of hound dogs since birth and currently hangs with his German short-haired pointer, named Cactus.

Music and literature, as well as films, photography, and art have always been integral parts of his life. Although he has been writing for over 20 years this is his first stab at making a profession of it. He spent 28 years as a married man, but is now alone, He sincerely hopes you enjoy his book.

FOREWORD

Throughout the years I have had the privilege to spend time with the author throughout his life. On the backs of motor-cycles, through the consuming of spirits, through the lens of independent film making, and just good old "hanging out" as friends do. I watched this man and his journey through life, from time to time, his ups and his downs. There are others closer to him than I that can tell you that the author has strong beliefs in family, brotherhood, and the liberties of life. He says what he believes, says what he writes, and writes what he says.

In the winter of 2010 his life hit me dead in the face during a visit to what he calls "his longhouse" along the banks of the Ontiahantague' in Upstate New York. It was during this visit that I realized, and I think some of his inner circle of brothers did as well, that we are going to lose him.

Joel had hit the bottom of life's well and I knew in my heart that he would take his own life before the arrival of spring of 2011. Not due to drugs or alcohol but from a shattered, broken and lonely heart. His heart is the biggest I know. Now if you have ever been in a situation where you know someone is in a state of no return, "helpless" is a word that comes to mind.

During the visit I read a short story he wrote for a biker mag-azine, it was very good. I also remembered that throughout his life he had always wrote his thoughts on to paper. I first read his writing in 1992 and that is when the title "The Incoher-ent Ramblings of an American Madman" came to life. Looking across the table at him I could see the exhaustion in his eyes and depression in his very soul. Instead of the strong, tanned, muscular, biker I knew him for... all I saw was a lost, broken man. This will not do.

It was at this point that it struck me to get his writings pub-lished, which would in turn get him focused, get him to realize there is nothing greater than one's own life, and to get the worst winter in 30 years behind him and get him back on his iron and back into the wind... where he belongs. For those that don't know, getting a book published is harder than finding an honest politician that doesn't lie. I told Joel we needed to do this and get his writings to the masses. I found a self publishing company and the rest is history.

From time to time you will see notes from me to you... the reader. The notes are there to help you along on your journey into the mind and the life of the most honest man I know. It's all in here just as he wrote it. I have asked the publishing company to not edit his writings as they are ramblings, poetry, philosophy, self help and stories. It's uncut, raw and it's all in here... life, love, and loss. I hope you enjoy his writings and if you don't... well... we don't give a shit.

Todd Michael Sullivan, the German

Dedication

To my Mom and Pop: Earl Stewart "Stew" Waterman Jr., and Catherine Susan Waterman. A man couldn't ask for better parents.

To my Brothers; James, John and Jeremy. For tolerating me throughout the years.

To my Ex-Wives; Ili, Julie, Rainy, and Kiyomi. You gave me a life time of Ecstasy and Agony.

To Jacqueline Janet O'Bey...my first love

To Hollywood; You're the Laughing Man in the Devil Mask.

To Biggin; Shot and a Beer... Bro.

To Stitch; Thanks for always being there.

To the German; I can't thank you enough old friend. "The eyes and the ass!"

To Josh "Jesus" and Cristin "Roxy" Bockman; Heartfelt thanks for your remarkable artistry in all forms.

To Dr. Jay F. Sullivan; "My Brother from another Mother".

To all my brothers, sisters and friends in the wind.

To Jim Morrison and the Doors... many thanks.

To Natalie Joelle, I love you like you are my own.

To my hound dog, Cactus Boy. A friend through thick and thin.

And lastly to the ghosts of my fallen brothers, Rusty and Sig, every day is not the same without you, your spirits drive my soul.

PREFACE

It was a massive transition in my life when I began these writings. Due to no one's fault but my own, I had just lost everything. My wife and stepdaughter, my log home in Kelowna, British Columbia, and also it seemed that I had perhaps lost my mind. I was on my way back home to Upstate New York in my 1968 Dodge pick-up that I had recently purchased in Tucson, Arizona. My old hound dog, Biscuit, my constant traveling partner, was riding shot gun.

I called ahead and established work on a drilling and blasting crew through my youngest brother "Bear". I figured if I wasn't working I'd be dead, real quick. I was 29 years old. To elaborate on the extenuating circumstances that got me to this point in life would be a very long book. It will be, but I will keep this preface brief. With everything that had happened, somehow, something deeply buried and lost inside my ancient dark carnal soul was about to be awakened.

It was during this time that the "Incoherent Ramblings of an American Madman" came to be. With an unrelenting fury my mind and spirit danced with my pen hand. Some nights the dance was so frenetic that I would black out during the middle of the ramblings, and upon re-entry be literally astounded at some of the out pouring, It may have to do with myself re-introduction to drug and alcohol rampant consumption. Probably, definitely had some bearing on things at the time.

I had been clean and sober for a decade prior to that, I have always liked to see both sides of the coin... so to speak. But that was then and this is now. I hope that everyone who journey's into the "Ramblings" takes away something of benefit. This stuff is pretty fucking raw, so we'll see where we go with it.

Joel Scott Waterman "Spartacus"

FROM THE TRANSCRIBER

What you are about to read is 20 plus years of material that was written in notebooks, scrap pieces of paper, napkins in bars, and any material the author, a biker, could get his hands on. When a thought came into his head he felt the need to write it down, a unique gift to say the least. As the transcriber, it took some time deciphering and transcribing his work as it was in no particular order. The author strongly wanted his material transcribed as it was written. I had to convey this request to the publisher, to leave it unedited. I told the author that it is confusing at times and that I added notes from myself to the reader to help them along.

The author doesn't care if you "get it" and that those who do "get it" are his people who find joy in the pursuit of liberty and happiness. Such as bikers, poets, and artisans who lose themselves in the arts and cultures of mankind. People who tend to explore the inner workings of their inner selves may understand what it is written in these pages. If you have ever given your all and ended with nothing then this book is for you.

I certainly hope you find joy in this manuscript as I have. It is unique as it is not a novel. It is a mixture of ingredients of self help, self exploration, poetry, philosophy, and a journey though life, loss and love. Welcome to the "Incoherent Ramblings of an American Madman".

- The German

The Ancient Shadows Within

Chapter 1

I have a valued name amongst the dregs of humanity, but who in fact may decide such conclusions. Let me show you where we stand in the dark scope of reality. May my thoughts flow freely until I am empty and continue to flow from my core of insanity. Many years I have lived and many years I have existed, experienced various angles of perpetual thought and bizarre coherence. Mine is an energy untapped and ever furious, spinning, whirling, changing, challenging. Silken thighs caress my eyes I want to have even more. Sensual, passionate, mystical, violent. Everywhere and nothing, a continuation of being, laughter, sorrow, anguish, and delight. Thoughts of savagery and other dimensional voyages through the constantly scrambled experience of death, loyalty, and then some. Produce beyond expectation. Achievement of the giants. Look at me now, different yet typical. Tell me of normal and I will show you abstract, everyone coping in their own little galaxies, zombies, and weirdoes, freaks of malfeasance. Sunrise and cloud bursts on a quiet winter's night.

Metal and mercury moving inside of me. Flowers and sweet scented feminine hair. Passionate hips and healthy young bodies, smoothing the path to my twisted mind's lair. Centuries old my, my thinking of frenzy, ask if I have been here I'll acknowledge my time. Expect from me what you expect, but I will always have a much broader realm and blazing horizon. I have been to the most distant outposts of puny human understanding. Take from this what personally benefits you or tickles your ears. Permanence of the elements runs in my arteries. I am drowning on fire. Get these people off me. Come on, come on, get me down from underneath this dark and foreboding malice that is pushing me further and closer to the edge of self discovery. Who can open the doors for which I have no handles? Do I have the handles? What are handles?

Baking ocean of raw and unharnessed emotion. If myself will let me, I will continue. Books of expression stretching endlessly across the globe of my mind, my toxic paradise mind. Let me, let you, share forget too. Too much stress inside my brain., mountains, rain, mountains, rain. The difference is within us all! The killer awoke before dawn but he already had his boots on, I am his boots. No one knows who anyone else is. We are all aliens in a foreign land. Who does not miss the pleasant and magnificent simplicity of a fine gun dog? I have no life if there are no hound dogs to enlighten me.

Wisdom lies not with age, but with a broad experience in the full spectrum of reality. The wreckage of my past keeps haunting me, it just won't leave me alone, I still find it all a mystery, could it be a dream? As the Ozzman says "the road to nowhere leads to me". I have given up the best possible finery for selfish lustful desire, and physical pleasure overload when I already held such things in my possession.

When people look at me or come into my presence they may very well see a unique source of entertainment. More incoherent expressions of brain damage to follow after regeneration through sleep. The clock keeps ticking as the planet engines pulsate. I have become a hollow directionless corpse being manipulated by a dark and diabolical force know as myself. I've already been there and I'm very tired. Can you relate?, elaborate? Desecrate? Infiltrate? Or annihilate? New World Translation Bible: "Who will rescue me from this body undergoing death? Miserable man, that I am. "Have you ever been to the ancient shadows within yourself? I have but they are still not completely clear to me, perhaps they'll never be. I continue moving on to what I don't know. Through all that is taking place in me my smiling fox never ceases to amaze me with sincere love and natural, sexual, happiness, freeness, of beautiful luscious laughable spirit of youth and heart. We have been lovers for hundreds of years. I can talk about everything.

Communication is essential for meaningful existence. I love to have as much sex as humanly possible with or without the actual act of doing so. Many luscious sexy women are drawn to me by the carnal, primal aura that emanates from my personage depending on my will and the extenuating circumstances. Friends tell me your feelings and with grave, somber, jubilant, realization. I am aware that we travel on different and similar planes simultaneously. Who really is the faithful toxic fire chief of tomorrow?

Television presents a pattern of mind control so subliminal, that people watch the confusion with a patriotic fervor. Sick puppies man. Where am I? and why am I? Don't touch my stereo. Get it! The greatest crime ever perpetrated is the forced cultural disintegration of the Native Americans. I am a 300 year old Lakota Sioux Warrior, Shaman, and my heart is captured by the past, and the key keeper of my mind. "John, you can't be serious about the destruction of the ice sculpture." "Yeah I am Joel, I like it, but they'll throw you in county, and no one will have enough bales to sell, to bail you out of the incarceration, "Well." It's not about money, it's about people trying to understand each other. Trying to understand themselves. Trying to understand. Since my captivity to responsibility has been terminated, I am attempting to express my reasoning to you, me, and anybody who is open to the massive concept of reason.

I have this really deep cavity between my ears, empty, and overflowing at the same time. Who did all this man? Perhaps I will put my face on the cover and it will be a hundred seller, thousand seller, in a cobwebbed crate, in my non-existent cellar. Sketches of life from different artists. My kidneys are damaged. Snow laden evergreens under an opaque sun. Perhaps, and certainly, the spirit of Jim Morrison leapt from his Paris bathtub into my accepting soul. Marcus Twain has a pink belly.

My level is continually fluctuating. Ah it's good to unload man. He's writing, he's in the middle of his mind, he's not ready yet. He's a mad scientist. He gets his haircut at the mad scientist barber shop. This is for everyone, and no one. I like your style of expression. I have merely two extra senses, and who will define belligerence. Perhaps it's just a ricochet flesh wound. I like Jane's back. There is no talking to me. Gimme my Newport deal.

A mindless child has removed my statement. Elias is a little bit off. I'm pissed. I'm not impressed. I'll drink his blood. Fuck it, I'm writin a book. It's a situation of mind over matter, if you don't mind it don't fuckin matter. Jimmy cracked corn and he don't care. Where have I been? Ask me where I haven't been instead. White rats and miniature English sheep dogs. Man you got big arms for a guy your size. I'll bite your nose off. Rick Derringer drove a 68 cutlass, and he didn't even know it. Spring fest several times, and I'll raise you with a couple of thousand islands. Moonlight helmetless rides, with a man who was part of his Harley fuckin Davidson. Off a bike for 10 or 12 years, and to ride Bear's hog at 90 M.P.H. with no helmet is freedom acceleration. Put the console out on the front yard, and crank Magnus Opus until your fuckin head melts. Drink all forms of fire water until your cranium collapses. Am I under the influence of excess you ask? 11:11 "Joel, come back." Do you want a cup of coffee? Nooo. Don't piss the big man off. Run bare foot in a lake effect snow squall to the Yankee trader. Rusty got a light? As I fell neck deep into a septic tank. Catch them salmon. Jack Daniels, Wild Turkey, Red Dragon, Green, Purple. I got mister natural, fuck you I got dragon. Get away from my daughter or I'll blow your head off. There's a lot of weird people in here man.

The Lost Log Home in Kelowia, British Columbia, Canada

I'll write a couple more thoughts. When I look in the mirror what looks back isn't me. First I need to unleash the last 20 years before I can express the first 200. This could be infinite. I love screaming guitar vibrations. What?! Rock me, alright, rock me. What is this bullshit man? I am totally irresponsible. I've stood naked in front of my front door to seduce , and induce an 18 year old darling, before she went to classroom every morning. I love humidity. I am a whore master and perfectionist of purple magic. Doubt me? Sometimes, I don't. Influence me no more for I have been influenced enough. If I could put into words the feelings expressed by a musical instrument, I would this day be a multi-millionaire.

Fuck money it's just paper, ink, and alloy. Let me go. We are surviving in a corrupt, and imbalanced environment. I love the deep grain of human experience, it's an adventure and a half. You can't keep it bottled up forever, unbottle it man, pop the fuckin cork, and she said "love me, drink me". A little rough at first, but so are diamonds. Once I get over the initial rapids, this project might smooth out considerably. No pushin, come on, take us out. Good night. Yippie Kai Yeah mudder fuckaa. What have you become but insanity on the run? Run, run, run, run, run, run.

Bell Ringers and Whoremasters

CHAPTER 2

I'm just warming up. I don't deserve JCMcD. She's sweet and clean as honey but at the same time the coolest, best, naughtiest little witch in my body. I'm not the only poor, rich, unit that occupies my physical carcass. There is an old, very, very old demon without a clear name, but a specific purpose, that moves, and shakes my soul with precision control. I'm bangin my head until my neck hurts. Sherri is one of the best lookin women that has ever passed before my eyes, but Julie rules me. End of 12. 1:40 a.m. is it them? Or is it me? I miss Ili.

Most of the people in my dispossessed home don't know where they're coming from or where I come from. No more, no more. There was a time, in my distant twisted mind, where associates were remotely my kind but they've all changed the way they unwind. A keg of Bud and only 9 free spirits attend. The rest are sleeping in their ruts of routine, the rest are sleeping. Unload. Even some of the men of legendary wild reputation can't skew from their established tangent. Where the fuck am I. People are lost in their own simple games. My flesh, my blood, are far removed from me, because they are them, and not me. I came from a distant, ancient, thinking pattern of obscurity.

I am the desert and a churning turquoise mountain stream. Most people perpetuate their own, mindless, insignificant, realm, and no doubt I am guilty of the same crime. I don't even come close to deserving my smiling fox, due to my maniacal driven tortured guilty self destruction. I am bizarre. I am a chemical, mineral, vegetable, animal, pissed off about the simple ideology of the people I grew up with. They have been nowhere, experienced nothing in my mind's eye, or perhaps everything, as far as they're concerned. Let me out of here, Give me a really solid saxophone to express my teased emotions.

Only those of my kind may, and will understand my diverse thought patterns. What did I just say. I don't live today. I'm going away. I am attempting to impress no one. Those who put on aires disgust me. I'm really turned up by tiger striped or leopard skin underwear. Ohhh silk or satin preferably. I'm a fool, and a king, and a king's fool, and a fool's king. Roaring waves crashing on rocks filled with seals of all shapes and noises. Grizzlies in the wild, face to face is what turns me on. Along with the "sound of a switchblade and a motor bike." Thanx Elton. If I could see my step daughter Cynthia right now, and hold her, and laugh with her, I would be content.

Echo, echo, echo. Throwing sticks to Dion in a raging thunderstorm. Animals' in the dryer, build another fire, smoke until you're higher. The ancient architecture of East block is beyond description. Smell the dry pines of the B.C. summer. 66' Volkswagen, broken steering wheels, and burning Monte Carlos, ramming speed. I'm a laugh. Tubing down the river of fear, and no fear at all. I have no regard. I love to dance. To tease the women with my provocative sexuality makes me horny and happy. My kind of lover. I love Julie. I love her, I love her, she makes me laugh from my heart. I want her and need her, lust her, desire her, adore her, I want to be her. Holy shit man the trees are electric. Herman Munster, 90 miles an hour from Ajo to Phoenix, in my 68' Dodge truck. I have to many things to express, and I fear I will fall short due to duress.

"Where ya from man?" "It's hard to say." "Touch his dick, and your dead." in the words of Kevin Kline. I terrify my mother. She was so contently sure, and confident when I attempted Christianity, but low and behold, I'm from the wicked sultry underworld of deceitful shadow. I can twist. I'm on the list. The murky mists obscure my fists. Bear has a sensitive feminine nose. My black rotten, maggot infested heart, is being eaten by subliminal crows with psychedelic clothes. Concerts of sin, let me in, move your body until your wet with kinky, horny, serious sweat. I'm a whoremaster, don't forget. Mad bell ringers haven't quit yet. Put up more money to back your bet. I'm used, bruised, abused and short fused.

Childhood was so much better than now. Even though I was scared of my old man's fishing boat on Lake Oneida. Ever have a pet raccoon? I do miss mine. For they are obviously cooler than humans. Try a Cholla Cactus in your heal if you dare Crow Agency, Montana you hear? Can you imagine what it's like to take off your clothes in 46 degrees below at Liard Hot Springs, at the B.C., Yukon border and swim in the springs until your lungs freeze and remain totally healthy. Whitehorse, go there now.

On the frontier, December 1992

I want to stop but I can't, and I won't, I was once on top, so say nothing, don't. My head's fogging up from lack of sleep, nutrition, and concern. I wish I had the guts to kill my evil self but I'm a coward. I'm mentally collapsing. I miss my life with my wife, my daughter, my true and valuable friends, my creek and canyon, my beautiful hound dogs, the peace and serenity of my log home, my productivity, responsibility, dignity, coherence, balance, a clean conscience.

My life is a fucking mess. Satan is devouring me, like this mad cannibal psychotic freak is supposed to devour me, and I not only let him, but I season myself, and rip open my own body for to expose my internal organs to the bastard for easier access. By being with Julie, I ruin Ilis' life, and turning back to Ili will fuck up Julie's life, I am an asshole, Sometimes I just want to be all alone, in an insane asylum, doing harm to no one, but

I have to have the companionship, and attention of people. It's so fucking ironic, and confusing. Wisdom has left me entirely. I have abandoned true knowledge, and am receiving payment in full, thank you very much, I feel like I'm out there from another planet. I feel so very different from everyone I know. That's because I am. We all are. Maybe if I have a lobotomy? This is supposed to be five hundred pages, minimum, but tonight I feel drained and empty. No doubt I need more drugs and alcohol to continue, seeing as how the last batch has worn off. Somebody shoot me. Please. Lock me outside till I freeze. Take a ball bat and break both my knees, stretch my neck from a tall dying tree. I then could call me, myself, free. I ran away from home when I was 15. I should never have come back or maybe never left at all.

My father and I wouldn't even eat in the same room together. I wish I would've never taken drugs, or never stopped taking them for 10 years, or never started up with them again. My own mind is the most volatile drug I know. Also the constant satanic barrage of world propaganda fomented by politics, commerce religion, military, and civilian misleaders. 99% of the world is under a spell. I broke out for a while, I have returned, and in terror I know of both states of being, and choose, against, better judgment, the spell. No one believes it. It's hilarious that something so simple, and obvious, can elude the masses of humanity. All in all, we are a very stupid race. My smiling fox reads me, knows me, impresses me, terrifies me, turns me on like no other, she is more than a mortal woman, possesses me, intrigues me, delights me, allows me, influences me and persuades me, scares me, devours me, I love her, I love her, she is so pretty, her graduation picture verifies this statement.

"The small of her back"

Her eyes virtually unreadable, her mind so perceptive, yet so in control, have I created her as she holds me in her power? I want her, I must have her, I must shed my guilt and regroup my strategy. I must gain control over the self destruction that envelopes me. Although I don't tell her, I sense she is already aware of what I am putting myself through. I want to stay awake until the sun rises so that I might say good morning to her, She is everything I ever desired. I love her mind. She is inside me and it is exciting and unnerving at the same time. I look at her pictures constantly and want to tattoo her image on my body, Her senior picture again I mention it. So young and fine, I want to die in her. Never in my existence have I felt such a raw passion for anyone or anything like Julie.

I wish she loved me like I love her, perhaps she does, maybe she won't tell me, she is love and in control. For no other woman have I ever wept sincerely or at all in the act of making love, she is love, we are in love, I love her, she move me, I want to kiss every single pore of her skin. I love her, She is mine and I'm hers and I must decide in her favor between guilt love and raw love. Please help my ridiculous uncertainty. It's such a simple decision, yet I fear losing her in the same manner that I lost my wife. I would never be unfaithful to smiling fox, but in the world there are so many men who would be much better and far worthier than me to satisfy this Queen of females.

My poetry is senseless, her sensuality is overwhelming. There is no one like her on earth, Why can't I deserve her. Because I continue to harm and punish myself for the destruction of Ili's life. She never did anything wrong to me. I am an extremely bad man, completely worthy of loneliness and self destruction. I cherish the pleasure I have shared with smiling fox and know she can have much better than me but her love is so sincere towards my undeserving soul. She is greatness.

My Iron Horse "Old Trouble"

Dirty Hands

Chapter 3

There has been a lapse, perhaps in my train of thought or naught. Pin it down to the wheel of karma spinning round. Have you waded through the buffalo grass on the palms of your hands and the tips of your fingers experiencing the exhilaration of your fathers? The sand, the wind, exists within. How old do you say you are? I am? He is? They might be? Many sunsets, thousands have I seen, what do they mean, smell the creosote bush in the Sonoran Desert. Hyperventilate in a 73' Impala, man. I need to flow, take me home to the land I know. Who is as old as we are?

Old friends and new acquaintances attempt to understand me, but I escape. Hummingbird thrill me with you complex brilliance, natures resilience. I can't understand my own hand, been given an ultimatum. Should I sing or relinquish everything? Snow in my beard and I feel so weird, so weird, am I unclear? So many birds have I heard sing. I devoured everything. Ask me about pain, some men predict me sane, I'll scream out "watch again", "again"... "again". Deliver me from my own eyes and ominous western skies. Last night oh last night, I, even, I had a date with delight. A woman, so fine, as intoxicating, as my sexy mind. Everything that I must hear, hung from her passionate young ear. We made each other wet, I melt as our feelings loved how we both felt. Passion is where we both came from, and dared each other to come. I'll have her and she'll have me. It all stems from destiny, and propensity. The vibrations and chemistry seemed to me nothing short of ecstasy. Echo, ecstasy, echo, ecstasy, lay with me, explode with me, envelope me, experience me. I have desired her, since I was a child. She has grown to sexual wild. Her movements are ancient carnal passion. Feel the sand in between your toes as I squeeze your nipples.

The pictures and images in my head are like Polaroid's that fell onto the slushy floor of an American car in the spring... a little hard to make out. I get pissed off when I'm too drunk to work magic. It's pleasantly tragic. My irresponsibility never ceases to amaze me, give me whiskey. I'm cold, have you been told. My rights are sold. I'm iron and gold. People have no idea of the depth of our psychosis, mine, theirs, yours, hers, clothe yourself in furs. I'm a survivor, cantilever, touch my fever, I believe her. Flowers and ashes, too much hashish. I'd like to, you know what!? My heart is a widening cut. What next slut? The tallest oldest trees on the planet have a very distinct aroma. Molecules in the air possess my hair and go a lot fucking deeper than there. What's it like to be considered normal for a little while? Kind of an elusive concept if you ask me.

Some people on a foregone conclusion assume that my brothers and I are alike. My brothers have no idea who I am and perhaps I know them neither. If we knew we'd flee in terror, or to the mirror. I'm old. Very old, Sounds silly to you in the back of your chained mind perhaps. Close your eyes and collapse. Fuck. Music is my special friend. My head has twisted round the bend. Dark green colors of vibrant summer, fill my slumber with the gray amber death of winter. Cancel my enlistment in the book of enlightenment. Take my name from the book of life. Where did this blood come from? Have you seen my wife?

My tolerance is unpredictable and the morning air is chill, delectable. What's happened to my land? At the stealer's hand. They've removed my band, which was vast as sand. White dogs command, I can't comprehend. Justice is malice in practice. The sun has come up again as I dwell continually on thoughts of my smiling fox, my sunshine princess, my echo... if you're in control, let me know so I can purchase a cargo of dimento. I'd like to be an innocent boy again and regain my actual friends. I am so alone here. My sweat is mine, and even if someone looks at you for the first time with a glance of distaste, it is merely their own shortsightedness and closeness of mind. Can you dig? I'm a pig, with a great big... I'd love nothing more in the world than to have a 24 hour hard on, at your disposal ma'am. Whenever you'd like to ride, slide, get high with a provocative sigh.

Some of my battle armor

The most important thing in life is raw, uninhibited, passion, between a lover , lovers, lovers of freedom. Freedom of mind, body, soul, destructive, selfish control, Rock and fucking roll. This is my uncle the troll. Did you remember all, the super bowl? Are you with me yet. I'd wager a substantial bet that your reasoning in a nervous sweat and you'd like to forget... what I write. I will not cease for lack of peace, introduce me to your tight young niece. A warm wind caresses my skin, lets welcome it while the full moon spins. Why I ask as you gasp, and attempt to grasp my controlled collapse. Lets laugh. Alright. Come on, ignite with delight until hard bodies fill your lustful nights, I'd like to think that one day I'd empty it all out, but it's not a human possibility. I think I wrote that down. Feathers, and leather, minds hidden treasures open your doors to carnal pleasure, Can you relate?

My mom's name is Hate. Tell her everything and she'll dissect what she can. As I took steps and ran across Hoover Dam in the middle of a Nevada desert night, my flight... I'm 30 and 320, I'm physical and beyond physical understanding. I'm contradict ability. I contradict myself so some say, are they on the same way as where I play? Cloudy mind disables my flow, this I know as my actions show. The giant sequoias in the melting snow. What moves you? What is it you say? Let's play. Where will the ravens fly when toxins fill the sky. Interesting and obscure conversation with a man of similar bloodlines, he has his world, I have mine, decisions, decisions, I don't forgive myself. I'm here, near, there and beer. Can I relate to anyone other than me, we'll see, Wounded Knee. I will go, do you know, ice, fire, snow. It's hard to pin down, I have an ancient past, a ricochet present, and a cloudy future, I am all things and nothing. Come along and scream my song, along, along, until were gone.

Timber wolves sing in my core, I need to ingest more, and more, on an ancient ocean's stormy shore. Adore, adore, life and death, intake spastic twisting breath. Is anything right or left? Think about it in serious depth. Alive, inside, have we arrived? Stop and breathe the icy wind, stop and try it once again. I feel hollow again tomorrow. Empty me out with your limited shout and I'll relate what my heads about. Or perhaps try. Prisoners of the system, slaves of the establishment, crushed bodies under government, where the fuck has freedom went? Regulate me until my spirits spent, Fascists, Nazi pigs of America and Canada. The white man destroyed my land, the white man destroyed my land, culture killers and dignity thieves all their words are lies of freaks. Disillusioned and filled with hatred am I. My spirit cries and seeks to die... The world is an insidious lie. Science, can it meet our needs? Who knows how my wild heart bleeds? People don't change, they re-arrange.

To drink, to write, small minds and physical mite, don't add up to much, we're out of touch with our creator, annihilator, anticipator. Wish I was sane, and in the game. My brain is lame, in pain, again, summer rain. Where are we now sacred cow? Look out, in doubt, with, without. My head is mine, all of the time, coming apart, ancient art. Where will the coyote go when the emerald rivers cease to flow? I know, do you? I think not. My blood is hot, because I forgot, what it's like to be one, set me free. Hehehehe. The left side of my brain keeps crashing into the right, reasons flight, lack of foresight. What's it like to be old? To pan for gold on your own soil, hydrofoil, hash oil, she's my girl.

Ancient chambers of darkness have not abandoned me as I weave around a nonexistent pool table. I stand in a bar, of people bizarre, and they all have their own tale to tell, I know it well, can you sense the smell of the end of all things? Awaken me from this dreadful sleep. The night is deep and filled with rings, Rings of endless nowhere kings. Alive, alive, I cry as the sun sets deep in the tropical sky. My own mind's eye breaths a desperate sigh. In the words of a genius "no one here gets out alive". and another, "oh, there ain't no life nowhere." "Breathe, breathe in the air", I lost my fucking hair, have you seen a grizzly bear... face to face? I have. No guns, don't run, stand still and have fun. Some people treat me like I have leprosy, but they're not me and will never be.

How large and deep is anyone's mind? Unkind, life, unkind. If I had a perspective considered proper, eye dropper, head lopper. Execute us for a day, let's play baby, you say maybe, I say now and again, my friend, my stonily friend again. Can't keep writing cause the liquor's fighting. Fighting thought, sold and bought. German and I also drink but I was drinking at the time.

War paint
Horses
Spirits run
Heat and Snow
Setting sun
Cry aloud with violence proud
On native land they place their shroud
of false heroes and Death.
Sit back, take a breath.

I like frogs, and dogs are me. Remove your eyes before you see how simple life can really be. Silence is the difference between a crazy man and an idiot stick, dig it? Many people deny my thoughts and expressions due to their own lack of perception, small worlds have they, they'll never say where my head lays or my mind plays. We are but a speck of insignificance in the grand spectrum of being, Swallow me. Think on my lines of thought, dismiss what your taught. Remember the wife of lot. Wet pavement on a warm summer eve, I'll never believe this life I'd leave, or any other for that matter, mad hatter, snake batter, thoughts scatter, simple clatter of a spotted adder as his scales spatter across a lighted bong, so long, so long. In Jimmy's words; "This is the strangest life I've ever known."

I've got a friend who went from New York to Los Angeles looking for his family when he got out of the joint, and when he came back to New York he got a hold of me again and the rest was history, or mystery, soon we'll see, what life might be, when our minds are free, from restrictive chains of predisposed ideology. Open our minds, so many are unable to do such a simply, difficult thing. Brain washed by politics, media, commerce, religion, military. Free your minds. Abandon and rediscover your ancestry. "Discipline yourself with complete freedom of thought and expression, cancel paranoia, caution is for those at fear of self discovery." Speak all that enters mind and heart to set yourself apart from those who deem themselves smart, for everyone has knowledge to their own degree. You are you, and not me.

Practice individuality. Most people are afraid of my thoughts and actions due to several factors. They are struck in very small brain patterns, sometimes I may be also, but to me this seems unlikely. I can communicate to all peoples about all things, to have a closed mind is to strangle and deny ones full potential for understanding.. Fear not what you don't understand, make it understood in every way you possibly can. Learn, learn, learn, burn, burn, burn, when am I gonna get my turn? Our world is so small and insignificant as a planet and how much more so in our daily personal lives? Specks of dust, ashes, and rust. There are trees 2000 years older than the oldest living human, still growing, and we have the audacity to think we are superior.

Man is the destroyer of all things beautiful and natural. Humanity is beautiful, yet poisonous at once. The most breath taking and intoxicating art work in the universe, women, sleek, beautiful women. No life without them. Man's best friend, a dog. A women's, diamonds. Who is brighter, honestly? Long is my absence from the pen, I'm wound so tight, on a window pane night. All around me is unglued, my mind and heart a bloody feud, my better judgment perhaps unscrewed. Quaaludes dude. Into your blues. Drinkin cold gin in a long morning rain might divert the pain, pour three more shots again, and sleep with my brain, Things are getting out of control, control, control... What has fuckin happened to me? Beyond all human understanding and reasoning is where I comfortably fit in. I'm thirsty again. I'm trippin. I should stay awake until they come for me. My hands are so dirty. It's 7:30. I miss my real life so much, Scott Lane. Help me in the long morning rain. Take a well packed journey on a trip of pain, Today was an immensely diverse experience to say the least. What a laugh, not.

Temporarily Derailed

Chapter 4

Scarlet Sun

by Trevor Quig and Joel Scott Waterman

Desolate Monsters of Energy
Churning Genetic Frenzy
Young Brown Bodies Entice Me
Confrontation Invites Me
Sweet Dreams of Passion
Blackened Night, Scarlet Sun
To Touch her Soul of Light
My Heart She Stole Tonight
Raging Violent Storms of Malice
Welcome Intimidation Chalice
Drink from its Foaming Draught of Violence
Push Your Senses to Limits Intense
I love your heart, quiet senses
You give me love void of pretenses
I hurt for you, do you for me
In the Scarlet Sun I long to be

Read my thoughts, decipher, identify my minds sniper and take him out with calculation, For if you miss him the first time I'll desecrate any further attempt with a brilliant fury of demonic reasoning and a mere mortal cannot hold up under the raging psychotic onslaught of a possessed mind, fucked and twisted unloading things not of this world. I am the tolerance machine, master of all substance abuse and mental intimidation and stimulation, L.S.D. has terrifyingly beautiful keys to all the ancient seas lying dormant in the human spirit.

We are here where time and space collide, climb inside and enjoy the ride. You can tear off your own hide where you peer into the dark side of yourself. Beer bottle upside his mother-fucking skull, get your ass outta this bar now or I'll dig out your internal organs and mail them home to your mother in a zip lock bag. Let's dance. Dance with the tormented one, I am he, master of spastic, chronic pain and romancing. My girl writes upside down and she makes my world go round and round. The world's most delicious sound is her passion. Her passionate moments of delight in the endless sweating night, Her mind and body tight, right as precision as a rifle sight in the hands of an assassin. I love to eat her and eat her right. She's my universal fantasmical sex kitten woman child. I possess my girl and we worship one another's poetic iconic sexual god ship. She makes the planets orbit in my eyes. I long to love her silken thighs. I terrify my mother with my rediscovered brothers of insane children in powerful cars. Try and keep up with me, ok? Touch this leather and tell me. Ask me.

Partners, you and buckwheat over there, and me and Beelzebub. There's been a lapse of about 6 or 7 months since I've put anything in here, but fuck it. My give a shit factor about achievement or importance or relevance is pretty well nonexistent. I haven't read my writings at all in that time period either so I couldn't even know where to pick up because I don't know where the fuck I left off. I'm working, I got a place with no conveniences an enormous amount of events have transpired since I last put pen to paper. Attempted murder, betrayal on various levels, confrontation, callousness, violence, and pleasure beyond belief. My sex life with my kitten is intense. I'm her slave and her toy. We've got wild videos. Some pretty good fights have come my way. Ask the dickhead fisherman from Albany who is more powerful.

There's been arson and laughter. Trip hammer. Bear is the best brother a man could ask for. Giant Nazi's removing my ears from Van Halen. Got some whaling tattoos, my minds to stressed to conceive raw blues anymore, it's a scary Shaman thing. What's going on is so fucking crazy. My main bearing is shot. Nothing seems to flow from my core, my soul, anymore. I'm uptight, unsure, and unreal. I really should let go and loosen my brain 10 or 12 notches again. I wonder if I wrote about my adventures on the frontier? Probably, it seems I've lost contact with my dreams. I got a few Christians trying to save me again but I'm lost in the smothering webs of the dark one himself. I suppose I ought to let this come natural cause it ain't right now. Later.

It's been a long absence for me from writing. It's now March 12th, 1995. The "Ides of March". My brain is hard as diamond and my balls are titanium steel. So much has transpired in thought and deed since I began this account of my reality, and I will once again attempt to record things of relevance and pertinence with some sort of regularity. Sobriety has visited me for 21 days now. Well so much for regularity.

"Opps"

October 15th, 1995 another half a year passes without events recorded. Mean season is fast approaching. I'm always melancholy this time of year. Lots of memories are associated with the fall and the approaching onslaught of winterland. Julie and I have been living in a nice quiet little two bedroom farmhouse on 158 private acres. We have made many improvements in our lifestyle as of late. In 5 days... 8 months of sobriety will be achieved. As insane as this may sound, sometimes I miss the mental and emotional torment brought on by my constant state of alcohol subduction. I'm like a leaking nuclear warhead, or a field of wild flowers swaying gently back and forth in the early August breeze. Been pumping iron in the gym since April, Physically, I look and feel better than I ever have, I suppose, mentally stronger also, I suppose. There are some fine looking bodies there for inspiration. I wonder if I can go the distance and make major physical changes in myself. Biscuit and I get along like old pals again. I believe that he lost my scent due to drugs, alcohol, and tobacco use on my part, not his. There are so many things I can't have and I don't have, and I won't have, and I want. I still owe my parents $1,200.00. The yellow truck from hell has a new motor and everything else on it is needing repairs. Working hard at the airport.

"I'M SPARTACUS!". O.E.P. owes me $5000.00. $5000.00. $5000.00. My old man went a few hard rounds with the Grim Reaper and came out scarred but still swinging. It was a very disturbing sequence of events for me. Things are easier between my mom and I lately. No one in my family will ever know me or understand me in the least of ways. Jerry and Laura created pretty little Jodi Lynn Waterman just over a year ago. When I'm near her and try to communicate with her I feel really soft and gentle and happy in my mind and heart. She will be, she is very special. I still don't have an Electra Glide Shovelhead. Rusty's brain fell out somewhere. Maybe when our common ground ceased to exist. At least I got 2 chainsaws now. A new husky and an old stihl. I'm a logger. It's raining hard and windy with lots of leaves around outside tonight.

Smells like October, 1995. It's my buddy fuck ball's 46th birthday today. 46 mentally stagnant years old. His ignorance, belligerence, arrogance, and lack of simple intelligence, never, ever ceases to stun me or infuriate me. Fortunately for his sake we are kin, if not for that I would have calculatedly , gruesomely, smashed his carcass into a bloodied twisted mash and feasted on his poisoned bone marrow. Wow, every once and a while flashes of demonic possession still plague my reasonable self. I know without reservation, that which was ancient was thrown back into the mirror, February 20th, 1995. Always, watching, listening, lurking, whispering, waiting... It's sure quiet around here lately. Sometimes I wish I was a totally gorgeous vixen sex kitten so I could wear all the naughty clothes of Frederick's and torment people's minds and hearts and souls. I'm insanely different from everyone I know. I want to be an Indian again more than anything in the world, but I'm stuck in the strangest life I've ever known.

December 6th, 1997 9:00 p.m. Write I must. King nothing, Listening to Metallica. Focus. Laying on my Hydra glide. Just want one thing OH WHERE'S MY CROWN. What a series. I need to flow, things are wild lately. It's been quite some time since my last entry but as of late, I feel a compulsion to record my twisted feelings with pen in hand. So much has transpired since I last took pen in hand. I am not smooth or fluent. Many events, sites, sounds, tastes, have I experienced since my last written expression. By the quality of my writing skills, the reader will note my progressive and imminent disintegration, HA HA HA. Get some, gimme some.

Biketoberfest, Northern Hemisphere, Earth, October, November "97" 20th Century. Madness, laughter, joy, smiles, interrelation, tears, dancing, reality, fantasy, friends, lifetime memory, solidly implanted on my mental tissue. James Sutor; Machine, man of men, man of machines, heart, body, soul, big man, alien, Nephilim, Wildman, friend, friend beyond friend, memory of Sutor can never end, teacher, wisdom, one of a kind, discipline savage! None can ravage him, Power load.

*Jamie, taken by cancer, with one of his many
iron horses, be at peace brother*

Lost My Pen for a Decade

Chapter 5

January 3rd, 2007, 10 Years After, What do I know? I find my-self writing with glasses now, how I've come this far no one knows how. I don't, I can't, and I won't. Loss, loss, loss of love gaining pain at a break neck pace like a runaway train in Lor-raine. A short time ago I spoke with "German", my brother of insane eclectic madness about independent film age and flew to Austin, Texas on a drunken mission of utter futile madness and experienced the calculated lunacy of "Hollywood". How can I let this instrument of ink explain Bull Creek in the pouring rain of a December Austin night of old school bikers stalking through such a furious realm of reality that no one can actually conceive such depth??? I wish that somehow, some way, my writing and expression never stopped but they did, they have.

Never before have I been confronted with such a devastat-ed period of mental subluxation, I haven't even attempted to write anything at all in the last several years for the furious consumption of fears, tears, beers and hot young smolder-ing rears has deafened my senses to such a maximum level of awareness that I really can't even be sure of my inability to write any fucking more. Can I? How can I get this all out? Rainy, Rainy, Rainy, Rainy, you fucked me; you fucked me up, heavy, ugly, heartlessly, so fucking what. Mad drunken drug induced, motorcycle wrecks leaving ancient brothers shattered, crip-pled, questioning, bitter, clouded, frustrated, empty confused, BROKEN... Those around them, since birth not knowing how to react, not knowing... loved ones betrayed everything that they stand for and stood for. What the fuck happened man?

The consummation of a brotherhood. I am so inundated by my own personal holocaust that I have visions of my father welcoming me at the airport of death while I wade cock deep in the blue, grey, and white washed heads of myself. My own personal holocaust, shattered dreams, loss of hope, lack of sleep. Lips and hips, my singer, my poet, my dancer, shut up, evil whore. Hound and cat, mother of all hats, travelin man, across this land as shifting sands demand my command of the damned, inside my wretched hide as I ride and abide with the disciplined tide of a motorcycle club? Racked with pain, gone insane, torn in two, blistered blue, me and you, thru and thru, holy fuck, damn bad luck, write again, gone insane, whiskey now, show me how, damn I stink, another drink, Stop!!! It was a mild winter that year in the land of the Kaniengehaga.

Many individuals were laid bare and to waste by their own personal realms of madness. Let's make some independent films about crazy fucked up stuff and such. Perhaps, "Happy" could star as a timeless, forever, young, wild, gentle, exotic, erotic, dominatrix, vixen, sex kitten, specializing in S.O.S. Perhaps? I have forgotten what it means to have fierce freedom of pen in hand. I must reawaken to reality before it's too fuckin late for me and I've got about 1 millisecond to open my eyes or they will remain permanently closed ha ha. How can I possibly discipline my wacked out mad self to write what's really important and what's deep inside of me????? I am such a massive American , human, demon, waste of furious, meaningful, twisted, carnal, beautiful, talent, talent, enlightenment, come on, come on, come on. I wish I could have everything.

I really want from the core of my carnal soul! I am eternally damned, sleep... Attempt to sleep and wash away the hideous nightmares of backstabbing betrayal! HA HA... Fury as you're aging eyes become clouded and blurry with... the Madness "GET SOME, GET SOME, GET SOME!"... All that I want is everything that I cannot have. What a fucking pissed off dilemma I find myself in, man. Dead face, briefcase, full of blues, full o human waste, demons taste, thoughts o haste, 10 years without o trace, shut up, fuck off, get off, come on, shut down, next train, flight is leavin town – destination, brutality... to fucking bad, don't ever call me again best friend, until the end till the end of time your soul is mine and for me there will never be another... lies, lies, lies, lies, lies, mother fuckin lies.

January 8th, 2010. "Hey, Get in man, no fuckin way, where we going? I don't know man, alright then, get some." Play some hysterical laughter brought on by an angelic choir deep inside the diviner sage bush, look out. Helter Skelter or so the Beatles thought... We might just make it back on track through black days, thru black nights , thru pitch black insides says James Hetfield. "The lost words were relocated in smoke filled chambers of Shaman conventions."

Footnote: All of my writings were lost in Jesus and Roxy's longhouse for 2 years! I had lent them out to read and they were "misfiled".

Nights prior they screamed out to my subconscious in a series of strange visions. Time is dragging and hammering by like a one-winged eagle in a vacuum sky. "Don't drink that bro, ahh no fuckin way, he drank it bro, he drank my piss... "

The ghost of Elvis is a slumlord and her Indian name is "Woodstove." She used to eat a chick named "Mudflap." When you think of something to say then you're going to think of something to say! Fuck this frozen wasteland behind door #2. Ride till the fuckin wheels fall off. It's an authentic Texas dance party with Seth Walker and the White Ghost Shivers. "You're cut off, go back to Jersey!" The shit is on bro! Mad miles a rambling not enough gambling, lives fall, a shambling, a trembling, staggering on thru and to what? Who fuckin knows, "screamin" who the fuck knows? Thanks to a fuckin mad mason, B.L.S. saved my hide. Runnin out of bridges, boiling up the land,, dark rift fast approachin, blood is on the hands, urines in the cans, forget your pretty plans, snort a few more grams, spread some tight young gams, slaughter all the lambs, and the rest of the fuckin sheep are surely fuckin damned. "That's awfully nice. Is it nice or is it awful?" Said the man with the ketchup and mustard on his back. Flathead, knucklehead, panhead, shovelhead, ironhead, blockhead, fuckhead, redhead, were all being filled with lead and bled till undead. Bomb the malls and suck my balls, let's chase the wind like iron hog men can my friends. I can't see myself inside my pupils anymore. So it's the end of line? Or can I in one last gasp attempt to recover what is apparently mine? "I'll see you... no way not another cavity search. O fuck bro, we need to find a lawyer in a van in the Round rock desert!" "There's fifteen feet of snow in the East and it's colder than a well digger's ass" said Mr. Waits. My current wife is half my age and has an impossibly, impossible ass. I truly love her Magic Face.

*"The Ghost of Elvis" a.k.a "Biggin" What a broth-
er looks like. Background: Pops and Evil John*

What strange and twisted paths led me to Magic Face? It
might have been orchestrated by the German. "You're not going to get me to Munich by fucking plastic women, Jesus" Ride
hard with no regard. Hey bro, Hebrew, the poor blacks, the
poor Jews, it's only the Redman who really gets screwed. Try
and find truth in American schools, good luck fuckball... ha
ha ha! These times and pages hinting, I'm your huckleberry,
get it out, it's overfilled, come on, come on! Ions of comedy
and tragedy buried inside me. The past 15 years have been
totally motherfucking insane man. Who the fuck came up
with this game plan?

If the opportunity arises to have some wacked out wizard or
twisted Shaman speak in depth or vaguely about days in "a
coma" or dark nights on the road with Captain Hollywood's
Travelin Freakshow featuring performances by special guest

bikers pull up a cold bottle of Yager or a case of puss to sit on and ask Jesus and Roxy to make a movie based loosely on the tale. Give it to the Biggin, he'll eat it! Show em your tits! Pokey, Pokey, Pokey, Pokey. 85 M.P.H. is Bandito slow. Ever been punched in the face by a Hells Angel, I have HA HA HA. Pack animals require my affection, and whiskey warps my intentions. I can't get out alive, give me your injections. Where are you!?! Let it flow. Aborigine I can't answer the phone... I'm writing. Loose fucking cannon. Get a fuckin grip! Are you listening? It's 75 in Glendale, the mad men are firing their horses, got a pipe bomb or a hand grenade? I'm closing in on something, what, who knows? Who knows, I broke your nose. Temptation, frustration, degradation, a conflagration of lunacy. I, I, I, I, I found my beer and its empty like a muthafucka. Small town rednecks are me, or not, perhaps it's insane but everything I've ever encountered seems dangerously insane to me. Are you frozen in time? Out of your mind, built on a slip-joint spleen? Log home bastard!

Defying the odds of your heritage in the brutal unending stream of ballistic time. Cry, laugh, kill, love, live, dance, puke, ride, ride, drink, fire, doom, freedom, sex, lust, happy,, fear, beer, oceans of insanity, deep and dark and endless. Who are you? Where are you from? What makes your raggedy ass cum? "Life, Birth, Blood, Doom", Zakk Wylde said it all. I'm gonna publish this as a book, this is my intention. I gotta go home, I know bro, we're just sittin here getting fucked up. We put up a grow tent! Bon appetite. With the prompting of Magic Face I watched a movie that may be a contributing factor into the picking up of the pen. Gay? Fuck off. I just want to pick up somewhere that I left off. Husband, father, family man, responsibility, Biker.

My mind and spirit is an endless battlefield. No I'm no angel. Where's that horrible friend that constantly lied to me?. Where's that horrible friend that constantly lied to me now? Ice fishing with her warlock step daddy. Jimmy's says "Some outlaws live by the side of the lake". I should smoke some pot, what have you got, or not, you're hot, you're shot, a lot, a lot, a lot. I just want to be free. Pictures and illustrations, I must add pictures and illustrations. Who's gonna run these high tech jobs with such personality, intelligence, and integrity. Give Spartacus a call he's good entertainment. The silly humans like his defiant soul. Black, sun, warm, frozen, happy, confused, friends, enemies, audience, put your kickstand down and knock the fucking piss out of a disrespectful son of a bitch! You want to see outta control? He's outta control. Hey Magic Face, you're the end of the line. Last girl I assumed to be mine.

I lost my train of thought like a mad dog and can't finish the poem. I've already written to you what I can or not. So many times I get on tangents that I'm compelled to call someone and I wonder are they on tangents compelled to call me? I suppose it's all happening in the fucking human condition... ... . "A tiny old Roman Catholic lay minister told me, as the altar boys were being sodomized by the priests and the wars and the sanctioned killings were raging by politics and religious deities that my leather jacket and vest were repulsive and she wouldn't be seen in public wearing such garments. I woke up this morning and I just laughed... YEE HEE HEE HEE and when I die I'll probably come back as a Sherman tank" thank Mr. Rundgren. Profound influences to say the least.

I just got off the phone with Madness, never have I participated in a such an oil and water relationship. Is it me? Is it you? What the hell are we to do? I'm writing. So I try to forget that it ain't over yet. Perfectly incomprehensible for the most of them out there. Good looking out bro, but those who know would surely never really let it show. "It's hard to say not knowing for sure. It takes a hard man to eat boiled owl." The "Scrolls of Joel". Layne Stanley has the voice of the devil, I have never felt such frustration or lack of self control. Fuck me man! Dirt.

I have never felt like this. Too bad for you traveler, you might want to consider and reconsider the time and place and circumstances you find your troubled, happy, silly, crazy, focused, raggedy, composed, ass in. Assassin, shit bird, biker, fuck ball, tin knocker, Shaman, demon BLAH, BLAH, BLAH, BLAH, BLAH, FUCKIN BLAH. Suck it up buttercup. How did this happen? It's back, he's back, they're back, you're back... .... continue. Demons, disasters, dichotomy. Listen. Listen. Listen. Get it all out of you, or not. Who's behind this? Where you been and what the fuck are you tryin to tell me you mad INDI-AN GHOST!?! Hey Joel, who are these new entities that you've crossed paths with in the last three moons? What's it all mean? Where you goin now? Way past the point of decline!! There's no time. Thanks Layne.

I want to carnally and physically tear my own skull off. What the fuck! Crazy, crazy, crazy, only the crazy sons of bitches know crazy. I'm not crazy. I'm primal, primitive, ancient carnal twisted, tortured, knowing, hearing, seeing, feeling, smelling, drinking, laughing, screaming, dancing, Writing. What is happening to us all? Where is it all heading? A collision course with dark and furious destiny, Wake up, look, look a warning! Come on, can't you all see it's inevitable and inescapable? Wake up Mayans, Pagans, Heathens, Ancients, Modern Scientists, Physicians, Politicians, Children, Homeless, Priests, Tradesman, Visionaries, take heed... it's on us, the mutha fuckin shit is gonna go down. Wake up or just gently apathetically non-complacently roll with it. Our parasitic conduct will come to a brutal close. Quicker than darkness.

Look to the ancients, the primitives, things only seen from the sky and the earth. We have all been warned for endless centuries. I say and write, wake up, but these are pretentious, bullshit, arrogant thoughts and expressions. No Seer or Shaman or Prophet, Warlock, Holy Man, Lunatic, can curb our inevitable path. Good luck you fucking bastards! HA HA HA HA. "Tear out your heart and see if anybody cares. Desolation everywhere" thanks Mr. Wilcox. Should I be driven on a rampage by the rediscovery? Enlighten me, frighten me, tighten me, smash me, trash me, listen to me or not, I can't write now without wearing spectacles. What a fucking silly spectacle. I want to love and all I feel is hate. How did the bad mother focused fuckers pull it off? The sparrows are flying at the overlook hotel. The chicken is in the pot. Trying to keep my head above ground, the cold wind is blowing me down UK UK UK UK UK UK UK UK UK UK I AMSK WHAT I AMSK. Hey Billy, I miss you everyday man. Rampaging reconnection, projection, deflection, masturbation, conflagration, situation. Misunderstand, because you can.

In $4^{1/2}$ hours it's my father's 84th birthday, this time around. Strangers will be looking to purchase his tall house today. Let's see what his grizzled old ghost does. I find it so increasingly difficult to express my level of freedom when surrounded by rampant, blatant, ignorance. Myself, I'm a mad Shaman, or so the Chinese will have me believe, we have sold out, no doubt, don't shout cause you won't be heard. Nazi simple mind set completely absurd engulfs reasonable, rational words you'll find more intelligence in songbirds... before the old Italians eat them. This writing flurry awoke masses of dormant energy within me. Let's see what the color of morning smells like. You can't top the dark, carnal, primal West coast ugly mind set and fury of Alice in Chains can ya? Stud dance... Maniacs in the Gypsy Joker Wind. You wanna see heavy? Hang with the Tacoma bikers for a few years and you'll see fucking heavy. Pulverize with sadistic might the Bilderburg Group, all day and all night. Kill them and all their seed wiped from the surface of the earth, before their birth like the blankets laced with small pox that they gifted to my ancestors. Death to the aristocrats.

We all better wake the fuck up and dump out our cups of ignorance. It's already too late, got second helpings on our plates and blind dates with sex crazed demons, posing as humans on TV, and in the papers and tabloids with contagious molecules that suck most of us in with a plastic surgery grin. I'm going back to New Orleans to relax now so we'll catch up in a page or so, later you sick fuckin biker trash bastard. Hang out with my father's ghost he knows where I can be reached. You heading out or comin in? Storm clouds of destruction? Leaving or arriving? Freedom, it's tough right now. I'm stuck in a snowstorm; cars broke down around the hill... The sound track of my life and these ramblings are to staggering to even contemplate conceiving. It runs a gauntlet that leaves the mind reeling and senses peeling off the shattered bone of rock and fucking heavy metal, blues, and roll!!!

You gotta live in your own head for a while in order to know what's going on. $^{1/2}$ these guys would fit right in if they knew, you've got 2 lives, livin, hit off both ends. A man who hides nothing, has nothing to hide. In my mind's eye my main priority is the wind but then reality comes crashing in. I should go back to school cause they're giving away free belly fat. Biggin and Chico are on their way to hang out with Saint Lucie and its Babycat's 5th birthday tomorrow. The very reality of real unrealistic insanity engulfs me so I'm attempting to sift through the ashes of stupidity and shuffle the deck of validity till my equilibrium implodes. What? What did I just think? "Birthday I would like you to dance, birthday take a cha cha cha chance... birthday dance." Thanks Beatles.

5.30.2010 I've been between ideas, smoking pot makes me very relaxed, "All the stresses of the day, get out of me! I can hear and feel the music deeper, the wind feels way more intense. Calling me into it. Farewell to my father's house. My mom is getting old. Stepping out with Madness." Give the dice another roll, Joel.

I've had a brutally rough year, moved back into my old long house all alone, my beautiful wife, Magic Face Madness, has a new boyfriend. She's only 25 and so is he. I'm 47 but I feel older than dirt right now. I no longer have the musical laughter of wife and daughter. No more pit bulls to keep my old hound company, no fish tank, cats or guinea pig. I've made a shift and rift as I drift in a mad loneliness, once again, pen in hand I gotta make myself carry on with this? The following page is a condensed (very condensed) summary of what I've gone thru in the year 2010. Although this page is dated 8.8.2010 (The day I moved back into this old long house) I write it on 1.26.2011. I'm trying to establish a time line for the reason in my slight change of writing style, the loss of my wife and daughter is like the proverbial "back breaking straw". The incidents that took place in 2010 have caused me to re-evaluate every aspect of my entire life. I honestly just wanted to end it all, whack myself, the big sleep, dirt nap don't ya know. But I've chosen to pull my boots up and carry on. The one direction I've been able to grasp is to finish what I started with these "Incoherent Ramblings" of mine. Finish this, my first book. It must be done, cause I've already started a second one in my head. I know that a lot of this lunacy writing jumps around all fucking over, but bare with me, after all I'm just an American Madman.

This was 2010. I started the year unemployed and ended it that same way, although I did work from March until mid July, for possibly the worst and most inept sheet metal company in existence. Started out the year with my beautiful wife and daughter, the three of us along with the dogs, guinea pig and fish, in hopes of buying my parents family estate that we had moved into Nov of 2009. By 2.2.10 my wife and daughter were living at her parents because we couldn't come together on anything. I asked my wife to leave and begged her to come back when she learned to show me some respect. She never returned and in July I was replaced by someone else. I'm still alone. During this time I was diagnosed with cancer of the tongue in April and went through two operations. After some blood work, I was told my wife definitely gave me some dirt. She and her parents had lied to me since 2007 and I uncovered all the deceit in July 2008, but due to my love for my wife and daughter and our family, I chose to love them and learn to live with what happened.

Then as the stress of living apart from my wife and daughter, the cancer, the dirt, and the horrible work situation piled up unbearably, I had 2 heart attacks in one week in July 2010. Prior to the attacks and the subsequent angioplasty, people had bought my family estate and after 6 months of being separated from my wife and daughter, I moved into a cabin at her parents that lasted one month. I moved out and in with a friend I've known for years., my bro, Stitch... a man built for porn. Then I had the heart attacks. My wife got a new boyfriend. I lost my job, lived with my brother, Evil John, a while and then moved back into my old long house that I've dwelt in for 7 years... 2 years, 9 months of that time was shared by my wife and daughter, Now it's just me and my hound, Cactus, again.

I write this on 12.21.10. To end this hideous nightmare year of my life in the same manner as it started is almost unbearable. I tried to help my 32 year old looser nephew out again, which as usual, ended in total disrespect and I got a separated shoulder out of the deal. Probably gonna require surgery. My wife served me with divorce papers in October, and I haven't seen or spoken with her in person since Nov 3rd when she had more divorce papers. The last time I was allowed to see Babycat was August 27th. I'm laid off, almost out of benefits, going to get screwed at tax time, and waiting on more blood work? My buddy Doc is an optimist. 2010 was officially a nightmare for me. December 31st I lost all my insurance benefits, thank you, the end.

Johnny Rotten and myself

"WHAT HAS MY LIFE BECOME"

3.20.1997

What has my life become?
Hard repayment for the things that I've done
I sit in silence all alone
What has my life become?

My pretty women far away
While her beauty dances, I work all day
How much longer must I pay?
What has my life become?

Feelings spoken
Actions lost, tattered emotions
Painful cost
What has my life become?

Words she wrote
Cards and notes
My heart is swollen, it blocks my throat
What has my life become?

I want Rain bad
It makes her mad, best love I've had
Can't get more sad
What has my life become?

"REAL HAVE MERCY"

3.22.1997

A few months ago, from this lonely today
Some real have mercy came walkin my way
Well she passed me up two times before
But now we share keys to the same trailer door

Well, when we started out, and decided to share
We both felt sure, we're a hell of a pair
Now she's in Dallas and I ain't there
Lately I'm not sure if she even cares

It's 2:00 in the morning, and though I can't see
I know that she's having great fun without me
Just me and my hound dog here all alone
This pain in my heart, setting deep in my bones

I tell her I want our lust and desire
To burn up our problems in passionate fire
She looks at me hard with her perfect dark eyes
And my sufferin' heart gets cut down to size

Could we just give each other our all?
I'm anticipating her telephone call
Will we come together and make our hearts right
A few days from now, on this long lonely night... ?

"ONE PHONE CALL"

3.23.1997

"You're spendin your evening with countless other guys
And I'm getting tired of all the tears in my eyes
Tryin hard to show you, that I'll give you my all
But I guess you're too busy, for just one phone call

Call you at your sister's, to see if you're all right
Tell me you're too tired, you had a real long night
Table dancing for a jerk off, with some spendin cash
Makin me feel like I'm just a dirt poor piece of trash

Ask me if I'm happy, about just one table dance
I wish it was for me, but I think I haven't got a chance
Sittin sexy in a barroom, with men from wall to wall
But I guess your havin too much fun, for just one phone call

Wearin all my favorite things, for other eyes than mine
And you're upset with me for cryin, cryin, cryin
Are you being touched by a Texan so tall?
Guess I've been forgotten, not even one call

"SHE'S DANCING FOR OTHER MEN"

3.13.1997

The longest 8 hours of my lonely life
Away from the woman, I want for my wife
Cutting my heart out, her body the knife
As she's dancing for other men

Her face and her hair, far beyond compare
Her so perfect eyes, in sensual stare
Locked soft with someone's, someone's not mine
As she's dancing for other men

One foot away or 2000 miles
I'm not the one who's receiving her smiles
Counting the lines on our kitchen floor tiles
As she's dancing for other men

The hours go by in the winter night sky
As she passionately flirts with a Texas rich guy
I wait by the phone alone and I cry
As she's dancing for other men

Her actions and words, leave my poor heart confused
As I open a can of so lonely blues
Her luxuriant legs in her black spike heel shoes
"As she's dancing for other men"

She won't dance for me and my pain she won't see
She says that her work makes her happy and free
Is she arching her back on her hands and her knees?
As she's dancing for other men

The longest 8 hours of my lonely life
Away from the women, I want for my wife
Cutting my heart out, her body the knife
As she's dancing for other men...

"LIE TO ME"

2006

Leave me, hurt me, hate me, wreck me
Please me, flirt me, bait me, sex me

Lie to me

What'd you say, gone away
Never leave, don't believe
All the others, never me!!

Lie to me

Smash me, bash me, shout me, out me
Kiss me, thrill me, love me, Kill me

Lie to me

Never be what you say you'll be

Lie to me

Abandon me
Can't you see
How you lie to me?

Not quite sure when this all began,
My life's being smashed by the devil's hand,
I once was a stone, but I'm turning to sand
My hearts been burnt with a broken brand

"Your words"

Date unknown

I play your words, again, again
I know I'm such a fortunate man
You are my lover, my best friend
I play your words, again, again

I want your voice, your flesh, your mind...
I know we're both the sensual kind
My eyes drink up, your perfect "10"
I hear your words, again, again...

Rain, I want you here and now
My lust for you, I swear, I vow
I'm different, love, from other men
Your words so sweet, again, again...

You claim that you don't understand
My needing you because you're grand
Our names in marriage, you say when
Your words so sweet, again, again...

"LAST NIGHT"

2.22.2007

Last night, last night
Such sweet delight
The mood was hot
Our hearts were right

Last night, last night
We shared such love
We fit each other
Like a leather glove

Last night, last night
Your taste so sweet
I love your scent
Your sensual heat

Last night, last night
You thrilled my mind
Tonight, tonight
What lust we'll find

There was a time when I was on the road rollin like a mad hooligan, thunderin, drinkin, dancing, laughin, fightin, fuckin, and so on. One night at Sig's Tavern in Tillicum, Washington, my smoldering hot psycho love and me were minding our own god damn "biznez" when Iron Horsemen Bam Bam and Prez. of the Outsiders, Tacoma chapter, Ed Wolf said "Hey Spartacus and Rain, you wanna take a ride up to Elbe? We said fuck ya man as we hammered shots and beers, laughed, and drank. So we fired up our shovels and knuckles and the 1 percenters out road me with Black Cloud following in his Indian wagon, welding gloves furious Rainier destination to Billy Bucks Gypsy Jokers birthday.

Couple of my 1% bros from Seattle, Washington

We danced and laughed at the base of a sacred mountain. Rainy was the most beautiful girl that existed in everyone's world at the time, her smile, her fire, her ass. She was my wife. So we were hammered, dancing, stepping into an unknown realm and we had each other full of arrogant confidence. The next day at the Highlander in Ashford, people of a different mindset were disturbed by the level of freedom in our traveling party. Heavy exchanges ensued. Moons down the road I almost lost my thumb in a stoned whiskey drunk incident on an abandoned Nisqually River cable car. Ha Ha Ha I have to do all in my power not to stop this writing. Several times, I spent mad evenings spending times like a lunatic shovelhead, "You had to fucking be there man." I have so many insanely incredible thoughts observations and experiences to pour out of my soul about life in the real lane Acoma, Washington from 1998-2001. It's almost a drunken blur.

Ratchet's corvette on the final t-day. Kicked out of the Puyallup fair for individual appearance? The pigs were scared. Coles, Fu Shung, Dawson's, Cloud Nine, and 48th Street owned by Rainy's uncle and aunt, Rainy... chasing her through the streets and catchin her cheatin on me in a Casino on Hosmer, pistols and shot-guns loaded lookin for vengeance. Billy was right there, shots fired, parking lot, gun fight, 51panhead. 1st time hand banger attitude crank in the bath tub. Giant beautiful meaningful visits from East Coast friends and family got it all on fucking film. Uncle Richard, Aunt Mary. Stillicum Blvd, Local 66 Joel's Brain, Mexican Larry, 6 and Nikki, Speed, None run, milloonium, Cresent Bar, 3-Somes, Maniac and Billy.

Old Biscuit disappeared chasing cats and fast food into a liquor store rescued by strangers and found by an ad in the office, after Rainy bloodied my face in an upset outrage. Go way back in time. If I were myself I wouldn't even expect or attempt to understand myself but I'm just fucking with me and you and every fucking body!! Ha Ha Ha fuckin Ha. I have ions of endless monstrous time to somehow express my blah, blah, blah. How many mad journeys will it take in this time to convince you that you need more mad journeys? Are ya hungry?

The Haunting

Chapter 6

1.17.2011. In my spiraling state of mind; loss, loneliness, emptiness, loss and lack of purpose, haunted by dreams again and yet again. The only time I can see, touch, speak with, interact with my wife and daughter is in my dreams. Magic Face has chosen yet again on a deviate course of action. Shut me out and off from all access and contact with the small of her back and the laughing songs of Baby Cat. I have never in all my existence teetered on the brink so unbalanced. I've been jailed, derailed, sometimes morally wounded in love and life in my mad, grizzled, inconceivable past, but the present current level of callousness, betrayal, lies, deceit, and treachery have snapped places deeper in my mind that have ever been reached before or perhaps I'm just reliving pain in a deeper more vulnerable state of being?

I just want to sleep. Sleep without dreams, sleep without breath, sleep without dreams, eternally. The only reason I'm still here right now is to feed and water my dog and let him in and out of my longhouse. I can see nothing beyond those simple, redundant, miniscule, lonely facts. I've seen depression before, but not on a level as dark as this, I don't want to see this shit anymore. Is it subconscious suggestion or pure mind loss trickery that unleashes these dreams on my exhausted heart? In the broken hours of last night, Natty Bo Batty, pulled my beard and held my leatherneck tightly and my eyes swelled with blinding mad tears and she said "I know Daddy, I miss you too". Magic Face stood back with a crowd of young faces I'd never ever seen and her boyfriend tried to speak with me but I had a shield of pain surrounding me so thickly that I heard no words and dismissed him with a casual backhand. She asked if I still loved her and Babycat but I couldn't speak. Her eyes, face, hair, and hips were to close, so close, I couldn't breathe, much less speak. I woke at 3:45 a.m. and dozed off again when the Grey light of winter's empty morning filtered into my dead eye sockets, only to be beaten up by more dreams. I can't take this anymore. Does anyone see? Or hear?, know, or understand what is enveloping me? Please someone help me, before there is nothing left of me to help? I am repeatedly being forgotten. What cruelty is this that I can't see or taste or touch or feel anymore. All is anguish and torment these days.

1.8.2011. Last night's dream was very intense. It started in a city somewhere. Your step father said something to the effect that you still love me and wished I'd take you back. I chased your car, a beat up Volvo wagon with plastic over the driver's window. You were wearing a platinum blond wig. I was on my bike and pulled the plastic off and you took off your wig. I said "Can we please talk" and you said "yes". Next we were in a basement of some sort taking a shower and you said "lets kiss like our first kiss". We slowly embraced. I cupped my hand softly on your head and you moved it away saying "no, not like that". I squeezed your tight young ass with my right hand and you did it again "no, not like that". We kissed so tenderly and you got back in the shower. You wouldn't take your panties and bra off. We got out of the shower. I said "why don't you take your clothes off". You replied that you "hadn't worn a pad in days". Then you put on a sexy little coat, hat, and tight pants, grabbed a squirt gun and said "Let's go". I said I needed a gun but there wasn't one. So I said "I'll just stay behind you and throw rocks then". We left the basement and entered the sunny street above. Then I woke up. I t was dark at 5:00 a.m. I was still alone. But we kissed...

12.3.2010. Last night I dreamt of you, sitting in a chair with my favorite pants on and a tiny little top accentuating your muscular young frame. You had a cardboard box on like a vest of sorts, open in the front. You beckoned me to come hold you. I asked you to stand. You said "no, come to me." I knelt between your sexy young thighs and embraced you. I wrapped my strong tattooed arms around your tiny little torso. Tightly pulling you close, you smiled so genuine and held my face and head in your hands caressing my tortured skull. I buried my face in your little neck and sweet perfumed hair and wept tears of exhaustion. You gently pulled my head back and kissed my eyes, nose, forehead and nuzzled your breath into my old grey beard. Softly you spoke, "I'm sorry, I was just testing your strength and I'm coming home now." My mind and heart was at the point of exploding with relief when I awoke alone, got out of my empty bed to piss out the day's alcohol and could not return to sleep because I'm haunted by dreams.

I arrived at the long house of my younger self on the scared burial ground of moons past and was overwhelmed by a sense of malice and dark foreboding wrong. Stepped out of my cage and walked towards the entrance. There I was met by your screaming hurtfulness to "get out, leave", looking past your angry twisted face , my ears enveloped by your hateful tirade, I was met with disdain and callousness by my spirit friends accompanied in the back ground by two twisted dirty old demons in the shape of supposed in-laws shouting "leave now you silly stupid old drunken fool". "There's no place for you here anymore". I woke soaked in sweat, blind with loneliness and betrayal, haunted by dreams, unable to shake them, waiting for the morning light, empty and tired. Haunted by dreams.

1.5.2011. At 3:26 p.m. on my 19 minute fast clock I saw Magic Face bringing Natty Bo Batty home from school. The mind shattering influence from a Shaman's perspective. Laugh at you??? You know what I need? A clutch and a throttle. I ought to be Billy Man!?! Look at them go!?! What are they??? Gin monsters??? Visibly shaken are we.? The blue star, the dark rift, never see me again, holy, holy, holy, holy fucking bullshit man. The shovel head could never fucking lie to me. My wife and step daughter. *Transcriber's Note: Most of this page was unreadable rage. Page 30.

Magic Face, on 1.4.2011 I passed you in traffic. I desperately can't breathe without you. I saw your Magic Face in traffic. It was 3:36 p.m., and I saw your Magic Face in the windshield as you transported Natty Bo Batty back to the land of the damned. 1.8.2011 = Torn up at a loss, heavy fucking metal, denim and leather brought us all together, Shut up to me! My mad, mad, mad Magic Face!!!! Remember our romance? Sorry we got on wrong paths, girly pants, how do I spell pants? Romance paths what's it's tight and alright? Send a birthday card to Natty Bo Batty. Who will understand? What do you want to do? Kiss your wife? She is callous, I leave you to yourself, West Coast. I can't even comprehend my level of degradation. Ha Ha. Fuck off Joel. Have at it.

HAUNTED BY DREAMS

1.18.2011. It's Babycat's 6th birthday and it seems once again my whole night of restless sleep was spent dreaming of Magic Face and Babycat. I got to hold them and kiss them, talk with them and just be with them. False and Fake were also there. Why is it that the only time I don't dream, is if I'm so hammered I can't? I hate what my life has become. I am very unhappy and have never been so lonely and without purpose in my life. I've got nothing to do and no one to do it with. I can't seem to muster any sort of productive drive or direction. I've never been in such a horrible limbo state predicament, I have survived horrendous blows during the demise of my past relationships, deep, wrenching, anguish,\and pain, but this time it is so different. In the past I always had some sense of hope. Hope, and a knowing in my carnal soul and the center core of my mind and heart, that something would give, that opportunities in love and life were waiting out on the horizon. Magic Face has left me with nothing of the sort. Sometimes it seems as if she has mortally wounded me intentionally? Should I let her get away with that? I oughta just lash out and lay her world and happiness to waste and sue her parents for everything they own, right? I am lost and despite all the hurt and meanness she has dished out to me. I still love and want her because of the really good qualities she showed me? I am a fool. I am Shaman. I am foolish. My life and path is better or worse, one or the other, decisive or without decision? Decision less?

Haunted by Dreams Again

1.22.2011. We were in Josh's car. Cristin was driving, Magic Face in the passenger seat, Josh behind Magic Face, me behind Cristin, Holly in the middle. Everyone was tense. Holly kept rubbing and massaging the back of my head and neck and quietly saying to me that I would be o.k. and everything will all right. Magic Face leaned around smiling and extended her hand to Holly, saying "congratulations, I hope you two will be happy." She looked at me and gave me a thumbs up. I snapped, but composed I said "what the fuck are you thinking?" "There is no you two, Holly is just being kind to me." "Everyone knows what you've done to me." She is the first woman who has touched or caressed me in over 7 months." "I'm used to being touched by my woman every day, but thanks to you it will never happen again!" "You gave me dirt!" "What the fuck is wrong with you?" Maybe you can just go around spreading it with no conscience, but I'm not going to spread dirt to anyone. "You've made it so I'll be alone for the rest of my life." "You have ruined me." Everyone just stared at her silently. I woke up and immediately wrote this down. I wish none of it ever happened, that it all was just a really bad dream. I wish I could get it all out of my mind and heart because it is slowly destroying me.

Cactus Weedeater

Chapter 7

I cannot even fathom my weed coming up missing on my kitchen table. Stitch fed it to Cactus. Cactus... yea... you're a little high tonight. What was I gonna do? It's time for me to "get the fuck out of here!". I'm not gonna say nothing cause "You got to give me a ride out of here". You've always been welcomed in my food chain? Now what the fuck? Cactus, Biscuit, he's wacked crazy toast. "Stitch 1.18.2011 4:20 p.m. Wow, why, is my truck running? I'm in trouble. You? It comes back in hear, here... HEAR YE! HEAR YE! HEAR YE! That's some "wicked good" pipin hot hillbilly grub! "Write this down, having a dog ain't a good thing." McManus said. I agreed and disagreed with consciousness only I could understand, blues, blues, blues... enlightened my ear holes. "How will this be recognized???" as Hendrix confronted the night sky, and as my mind relaxed enough to write this, I found it most unusually, non usual and I at the throttle. "Real, real, real" I say. "What? The music The music, dance, sing, play mad tools of beautiful heavy... wait a minute... how can I even contemplate. Somehow or another us motherfuckers gotta get thru it. Holy fuck I got to get home, my level of consumption approaches dangerous... ... Look, look, look out, fucking insane lunacy, all destroyed effort. When will I learn, it's so fucking stupid, it's so fucking stupid, and I hook up with a maniac like you?! You're one of the trippiest mofo's I know. Hey, hey I love it here! I got a house times two. "Holy fuck this isn't gonna come out good." "Fuck you! Jesus Christ, I gotta quit drinkin bro!?" I gotta get her done. "Have you ever had the blues? I partied with your brother "Sprized" I made it thru? I'm in the cross roads, the cross hairs, I'm gonna break on through. Thanx Jimbo. People are strange. My old brown dog was partyin.

I heard Johnny Adams croon out "Even Now"... and I was sitting next Bernd "Sig" Wachter in a rundown 3rd floor cube,
looking out at Puget sound about 4:00 a.m. He was a little
out there on heroin sumtimz, but all in all we'd known one
another for centuries or so it seemed to us. Ha! Ha! Ha! Now
we was both ridin trouble heads for many moons a "73" and a
"79" respectfully. "Raisin Pie" praises and accolades, tits and
ass, shots and beers, rock and mutha fuckin roll. "GET SOME,
GET SOME, GET SOME!" We were building America! The hos-
pitals, schools, stadiums, prisons, malls, walls, and fences that
entertain and unnerve the masses... !! What'd you think... "it
was gonna run smoothly?" "Start rethinking soldier". If everyone, for just a split second in time could be comically genuine, then that might happen. Profound or irrelevantly pomp-
ous, arrogant, ranting??? Up to you, my words, may and most
certainly will flourish when I have departed from this stage
coach stop in dirty mad real time? "Glad I'm out of beer."
"It's wicked good when you run out of that shit" says I, in
an intoxicated, stoned, focus.

1.19.2011 6:00 p.m. Just took council with the German. If I am to
have a future, a successful future, even if all alone, I must apply
myself and follow this cause of writing, being an author, artist,
poet, photographer, film maker, singer, self. I have an opportunity that I can't let pass. I must excel or I surely will die having
achieved virtually nothing of substance or significance, and I
won't go out that way. I am going to become famous. After all
that has happened in this life of mine, I am compelled to share
my own twisted unique vision with the rest of the human race.
This must be done. Am I finally free? Or will I be... trapped in
chains of endless misery? We'll see...

1.20.2011 I've always been a D.R.E.A.M. Definitely Real Extreme
Ass Man. All my life I've ridden and been ridden by perfect "10"
heart shaped female ass. What is "superior autobiographical
memory" anyway? I have to discipline myself and write everyday as a job and career, get computer savvy and purchase the
tools I need to make this a complete success, oonie goo goo.
Another day of lake effect cabin fever.

1.20.2011. 12:54 a.m. I'm not quite sure on how to go about this
mad undertaking, the shaking off and breaking of my old set in
my ways rut conduct. All my life the best gig I've ever known
is having the side by side companionship of a smoldering hottie. I've had merely four serious committed relationships. The

first relationship was for 10 years, the second for 4 years, although this one continued sporadically throughout a period of 21 years, off and on. The third for 10 years and the fourth, last, most recent, unhealed was also 4 years. 10, 4, 10, 4? O.k. O.k. What's it mean? I also had many brief ones, when I was, as you say, "between jobs". I have been very fortunate to share life with these wonderful, beautiful, toxically harmful, monster friend/lover females. Or not... just kidding!

I will log some of my memories and experiences with them to perhaps heal my heart and ease my anguished mind. I've written an index, so to speak, of people, places, times and events to pull from so I guess I'll just ramble on from that. Are there any American Indian news people out there? I see black, white, and yellow in media. I'm seeing red without an actual red presence.

Insane mad dreams of my father and Sigman both have been in the spirit world for many moons, yet in my dreams they are still very much alive and dead... I love the texture of salmon back bone in my molars chowin down. It's nuts that it took me 18 and half years to write the first half of this twisted gibberish and six months to write the last half. My next book will take less time (yeah right dude). I have already made a concise and lengthy catalog of events in my moons on the road to pull mad tales of debauchery from. Today is my birthday,

1.31.2011 It was -12 degrees in the frozen wasteland of Upstate New York this morning. I'm gonna press on to finish "The Ramblings" out. Tentatively by 3.1.2011. None of us really have a lot of time left anyway (the "Dark Rift" don't you know?)

I'm figuring I won't be so lonely when this hits the shelves, but as for now I miss my wife "Magic Face" and daughter "Baby Cat" so much I can hardly breathe sometimes. It will be four years ago tomorrow that we first kissed. It's been more than 7 months since we last kissed. I miss her. I've been replaced. She has not. Lonely. Unbearably lonely. Just me and my old hound dog, Cactus. Rather melancholy for the most part. Well the entourage just rolled out, Irish Bobby came over for some pills and such, Rotten and Dawn shared several drinks and we smoked a fatty. Stitch was here, hammered with a newly purchased 1961 Model 94 Octagon barrel Winchester repeating rifle in tow. Couple of traveling meat salesman stopped by, one from Arkansas, the other from Pakistan. Slick salesmen.

My associates purchased $310.00 worth of meat. Being that is my whoopty fuck doo b-day I received many packages of free meat seeing how the business was transacted in my long house. Stitch took the meat men to his joint, Johnny Rotten and Dawn just split, and I'm going to dinner with my ma.

Thanx Jesus, Roxy, Sheldon, Zed "Mohawk", Persephone "Shaman" Bockman... For the hospitality "You gotta cut it out man" I belched at Wacky Cacky, a.k.a. old Cactus boy. Spartacus rolls in back roads drunk again, buckin the rules, questionin the establishment, defiant till death. Just makin an ancient point they were drinkin and smokin joints Spartacus, we're headed into mad territory in 2011. Come on, you gotta at least feel the awareness of the unraveling of the modern holy roman empire, U.S.A., ain't it beautiful?

Roxy and Jesus of Jesus Wept
Productions and Bird's Eye Bandit, 2007

What happened to Jesse Ventura's Conspiracy Theory television show? True factual journalism and reporting. Where's Jesse? Give me a shout you tough old bastard. I'm writin a book. Blues anybody? Anybody listening, livin, singin, playin, writin, thinkin, drinkin, cryin, dyin, da blues mutha fuckers "The Blues". Comin from all fronts, like vicious heartless cunts on a hunt, for an easy mark, target, romantic hard workin, lovin respectful foolish Madman. I miss their company. They have real pretty voices and the scent of their unique, hot, passionate individuality intrigues me, so I continue to want more and more of their finery. Why not? You got to get them to pay custom attention to your helmet head, and then you're imminently dead. Anybody listening? In the World? I know that a hornet, frog, crow, raccoon, coyote, wolf, bear can. They are listening and disappearing. The first people. What a bold claim to fame. All people's struggle heavily to claim this title.

We're an alien prison colony, hell on earth, a science experiment, a parallel universe, created and evolved. That's all well and good, or not, it might well be "The Planet of the Bikers." Valhalla perhaps? A mad ship of fools. Trees, water, and dirt, throw in a bunch of air. We can hang here for some moons. Then the new big empire crumbles. Come on man, it's not remotely farfetched. Who gives a fuckin shit? This prison colony planet is just carrying on life as we know it. "Calm down Keanu!" If we are not all in the Matrix, than the only reasonable conclusion to be drawn from this self questioning would be that "we are not all in the Matrix". Sometimes, though rare, even Indian Ghosts wind up in and out of "there". "Salvia", says sinister Shaman, I know certainly that the politicians and religionists, will interpret my words incorrectly, but "they" always been that way; historically. The ruling class are only interested in themselves. Liars, robbers, rapists and thieves! Filthy guilty, consciences. There's an asshole in every crowd, Don't get me wrong as there are some nobles who are genuine humans. 1-in-perhaps, 1 million. I'm likely wrong but I will wager a bet just the same.

"The Man from Water", birthday present poem from my brother "Joshua James" "Jesus" is wicked beautiful. You mad fucks will find it just below for your viewing pleasure. "They is mad artists!!!" Cristin Rose spins countless hours of artistry into me coat (see chapter " ") Then blast out 7 plus hours (more than that) on the WW II inner helmet liner of old "stew bellys" (my pa) his steel pot liner from the U.S. Navy pacific theater battlefield. Mad, one of a kind, only one like it on earth's face. a.k.a "Face of the Earth" Thanx Days of the New. "Only one under the sun artistry" Cristin and Joshua James Bockman. "Spartacus". 2.11.2011

Roxy's mad helmet painted and given as good trade gift to "Indian Ghost, Spartacus". All you wackos reading this drivel, might like to focus long enough to look and read "The Bike Riders" by Danny Lyon, 1961. The German spun me onto that maximum real expression of American Photojournalism, and free spirited writings. No place like the wind. Ramble into it at every fuckin chapter in life that you're able to write, Write it unique. Just yourself. That's all anyone of us can do. Good, later. "GET SOME, GET SOME, GET SOME"... back soon... Spartacus.

"THE MAN FROM WATER"

Once there was this dude who was swell
Who had a bike that was welded in hell
He'd ride on his Harley
Drink hopps and barley
And all and all was a pretty nice guy

One time on his bike as he rode through the night
He had an idea and what he thought was just right
He'd ride on his Harley
Drink hopps and barley
And do his best to murder the world

So he did what he said, he killed all the people
From lonely servant to the priest at the steeple
He'd ride on his Harley
Drink hopps and barley
And pretty much had a nice time

The day finally came with everyone dead
He put on his armor and racooned his head
He'd ride on his Harley
Drink hopps and barley
And occasionally howls at the moon

Dedication birthday poem to Joel Scott Waterman by
Josh Bockman. Copyright © Josh Bockman, 2011

Spartacus, "The Man from Water"

"HANDLE BARS AND CARS"

Chapter 666. I can say we met the HBAC crew. We're all prospects, we gotta be pissed on by pot plants. Fuck the pine needles man but god, who is this god you speak of, blessed leatherheads, Who are these newly entered madmen that I meet, eat and drink with today? Lou and Snake, they say "he comes into my town! Listen to this guy". Don't touch his writing fingers. They're like blotter acid. A friend will help you move, a brother will help you move a body, a pound, kilo, a dead hooker, a stolen horse.

You bought a fatboy custom today. This is Lou's chapter out of Melbourne, got pulled over trippin face called me and I said "fuck you man". What's the world come to when you gotta be on a cell phone 24/7. Oprah became a punching bag, draw it, $100 tab, no a $15 tab. Holy fuck, Ozzy's up there with 'em man. An evo motor with a margarita mixer on it, you're getting kind of gay on me now.

Come on Captain. Hey, we ain't done yet, get another piece of paper, these fuckers are sinister instigators . One can swear off heroin, we're gonna write this book, are you scared, I'm gonna take on the birthday boy. What do you mean your old? Ready? Come on Biggin, let's go, I don't think I did, did I? "757" Snakes band, so I gotta know this, I gotta hear this gunpowder cake, that outta twist your head. Wait... write that down. Tell the children to close their eyes and the women to close their legs or to open them. If I hear Zakk Wylde sing this song I will get it tattooed on my skin. How do you say "on my skin? Stitch..shit the birthday cake is all over the corvette. Do you remember old hound?

"Home, home again, I like to be here when I can, when I come home... cold and tired, it's good to warm my bones beside the fire." Thanks Mr. Waters and the boys from Floyd.

I'm so fucking sick and tired of giving all I can just to be lied to and shit on. The next broad that calls me pathetic is gonna get her fucking face punched off. I've never hit one in my life, but there's a first time for everything. Fuck it. I hate this god damn life so much for I am unloved and will never know love forever more.

I have been executed by a heartless little whore. My passion is dead, never to live again. Words of an angry friend. Got to get this to the German to unleash to the masses.

"House on Albion Cross Roads"

Written by my mother, Catherine Susan Waterman

March 1968

It was a cold wintry day in March when we drove up in the front of the house. It seemed at first like another part of the world. We had only left the city 45 minutes before and the streets were wet and thawing and the remnants of dirty grey snow lay all around, But as we parked the car well off the shoulder of the road, I wondered to myself just how long would it take for 4 feet banks of that white stuff to melt away up here. The real estate man said the house and property we were going to look at was in the snow belt and it really didn't mean to much to me at the time. Stew and I had been hunting for 5years for just a place in the country to raise our four boys. Jim, who is the oldest, handsome and lean for all of his 11 years. John, truly all boy and rugged as a 9 year old could be. Then came Joel, deep and sensitive with dark brown eyes and an apologetic little frown. Last bit nit least was Jeremy who seemed to be a combination of all the others but with certain little ways that were all Jeremy's.

The House of Waterman

As we walked across the road toward that big old white house with its green shutters we both looked at each other and in that minute I think we both felt that this was it. By far I don't mean to say that "there was our dream house" not by any means. But call it instinct or what have you that certain feeling that somehow rings a bell or does the trick. It seemed to have a lot of potential for what we could do with it. I had a mental picture of 10 years in the future and I honestly think Stew saw the same picture.

That was in March and three long months later it was legally ours, The boys just couldn't wait till school ended so they could move to the old house with its pond and 83 acres of, "as they called it, their own private forest and hunting grounds," It wasn't all that but to Stew and I it was security and above all was our own little piece of God's Country.

The Boys of Waterman

Left to Right: Goddamnit Jim, Evil John, Spartacus, and Bear Naked

The Great Union

FIRST ROAD TRIP

The year was 1894. No, wait, 1967. I remember it as if it were yesterday. I was four. It was summertime. The place, 100 Colonial Drive, North Syracuse, New York. Just up the road from the Spinning Wheel Bar. One of the curious details that stands out in my mind about that time in my life is when the pesticide van would drive thru the neighborhood, back doors open spewing a thick cloud of who knows what and all us kids would run and ride our bikes and chase that van engulfed in that thick white cloud of ... Like I say, "Who knows?" It was the 60's, agent orange maybe? No. It was for mosquito control due to the Cicero, New York swamp. Good stuff.

Anyway, on with the road trip, man. My Uncle Richie, a.k.a Dick Woehrle, a WWF Career referee, and my Aunt Judy, a real hot nurse, were visiting from Philly. He was actually my dad's second cousin, but we all called him "Uncle Richie". What a tough guy! Well, all the adults were doing adult shit and I don't know where my two older brothers were. My little brother was only four or five months old at the time so he was hanging out in his crib or something.

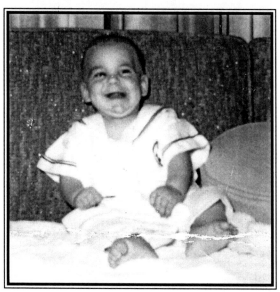

"Put that 12 gauge down Pa! Don't make me throw a right"

It was then that myself and my two best pals, J.J. Burke, and Michael Folger, decided we had enough of the monotony and the daily hassle of being four years old, so we decided to bail. We all agreed to bring my Herman Munster talking pull string doll along, cause he went, everywhere I went. In 1989, twenty-two years later I gave Herman Munster to my buddy Dean Nolan's son, Jesse, in Ontario, Canada before I set out for British Columbia which in itself was another long road trip. So anyway, when the coast was clear, we split. We headed West on Colonial Drive. After several grueling miles, actually just two blocks, we veered North. The next day, which was a half hour later, we came upon a fearsome and awesome place! There were these huge yellow machine beats that had ripped up great piles of dirt. There were stacks of giant straws piled up all around and orange barrels were everywhere you could see. The sun was going down and we were tired, hungry and scared. But we pressed on. Suddenly, out of nowhere, my dad and my uncle pulled up in dad's big Chrysler and said "What the hell do you think you're doing!?!" They jumped out and seized us. My old man blistered my ass and gave fair warning not to ever worry mom like that again... ever... no such luck.

When we got home we ate a bunch of cool snacks cause we were exhausted from the road. I'll never forget those yellow machine beasts. Many years later, I learned how to operate every kind imaginable for a company called "Orchard Earth and Pipe". What a great experience that turned out to be. I gained vast knowledge from them and earned a really decent living. I'm not sure, but looking back on the miles I've traveled since that first road trip I'm guessing that's when my wanderlust must've begun, That first road trip set my path in motion and I suppose I ain't quite finished yet. My folks gave me a strong set of values and roots, but I gave myself the love of the road trip.

Crissy on the "Snake Eater's" Iron

Sig's Harmen, Cresant Bar, Washington 2000

Biketoberfest 1997

In the wind at Sig's Funeral, Tacoma, Washington

Kate and the boys

The German and Spartacus

Johnny Czysz a.k.a "The Hydraulic Warrior

*Billy, Spartacus, and Hawk...Singing at
Sig's Tavern, Tillicum, Washington*

Spartacus and Cisco Foxx

Spartacus and Stitch, Trophy Hunters, 2001

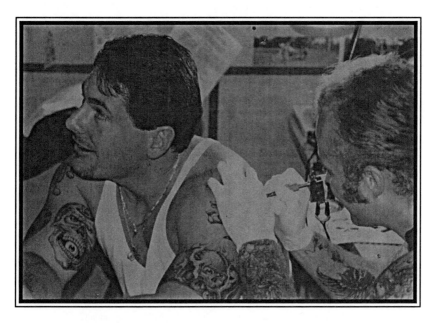

"Jonny Peach" ink'd by Jimmy B., at Spartacus's Longhouse

Boozer and H-Wood

Steve Keown, Johnny Rotten, and Spartacus

Richie Falcone wrenchin on "Old Trouble"

Mike Hazard, Winter 2011

Family of Artists

Jesus and Roxy

Just Nick and Roxy

Captain Hollywood's Traveling Freak Show

CHAPTER 8

It's the tasty blues, served up tasty by ZZ Top. Blue jean blues is music my spirit is always happy to muse. Reminds me of a girl I once knew named, Chrissy, 1980. Nice ass, pretty mouth, bedroom eyes, and sensual thighs. Then I leapt into, Cap'n Hollywood's Travelin Freak Show. This will be one of the longest and heaviest chapters in my writings of lunacy.

Now there was a lot going on in my world when Rain and I crossed paths with old H-Wood and Poke, the Hydraulic Warrior had recently been paroled from "maximum security". Wrong place at the wrong time I reckon, or not. I'd just got Rain back from her most recent tangent, April Fool's Day 2004. My bro "Goddamn it Jim" was fresh into the horse pistol (only hours) the night that she called from Jacksonville, Florida, wanting me to "come get her again?!" Jim got wacked by some 19 year old fuck ball kid who said "the sun was in my eyes and I couldn't see anything, so I proceeded to make a left hand turn into "fuckin go nuts" regardless. He smashed my bro's fatboy and his life into chaos for 20 months of recovery and a life time of "chin up tough guy" militarily disciplined biker Greybeard (still rides to Sturgis from New York). So I picked her up in Florida the next day. If you knew her, lived with her, loved her, were her husband, you would have done the same, or not, that's what old Spartacus decided to do anyway. Friends and family advised me otherwise, but I was and always will so fiercely in love with Eldoon (Rainy), You had to be there on the front lines.

So , back to there was a lot goin on, Ridin, laughin, lovin, fightin, drinkin, workin, payin, sayin, dancing, fuckin, cryin, dying, flyin, lots going on when we embarked on Captain Hollywood's Travelin Freakshow. At the time I was drinking heavy with "Ghost of Elvis", soon to be revealed as "The Biggin". The Hydraulic Warrior and old Spartacus had recently rekindled rampant insanity and wild conduct from ancient moons gone by, We were in the wind again, It was at Am Jam 2005 that we all collided in a Realm of Freedom; drug induced, alcohol induced, heritage induced... just happened to all be at the right place at the right time induced. Who really knows ha ha ha ha ha ha ha fuckin ha!

So here how's the road trip unfolded. The Biggin, had already set out on his Electra Glide Standard 2 days ahead of myself. Before we even rolled out (we meaning Hydraulic Warrior, Spartacus and Rainy) Biggin, Josey Whales, Eric and Debbie, and Rochelle had already struck camp into the party and Hollywood and Pokey were set down adjacent to these hooligans, Czysz (a.k.a Hydraulic Warrior) Rain and myself (Spartacus) rolled across the NYS thruway on our iron horses... destination... AM Jam 2005.

Into Cobleskill, NY we rode, As we blasted our way down to the infield, Rainy was so hot and fine. Thigh high lace up 6" stiletto black cum fuck me boots, sprayed on levis, cotton candy wind beatin blonde sex kitten mane. Full sensual lips, with a mad weathered laugh rollin out of her whiskey breath. Myself, in me buffalo hide pants (been wearin the same fucking pair since 1993) dirty, greasy, handsome bastard. Sun baked, my hide looked like the winter time hackles on a grizzly bears back. We were all laughin hard that day. In that irreplaceable moment in the endless, soon to end, stream of mad real time.

Left to Right: Spartacus, Rainy, H-Wood, Pokey, and Biggin"

"All right then" We all said, as we rolled in. H-Wood, Pokey, Spartacus, Rain, "The Ghost of Elvis", Big Lenny, Combat Veteran, Biker Hooligan (instant friend upon meeting), all converged. I was sun baked, weathered, grizzled, and full of life. Workin for Orchard Earth and Pipe, busting my cock on Boozer's blacktop production crew. As I rolled me old recently rebuilt trouble head shovel head towards the mad encampment of old and new friends this is when the freak show took off, perhaps? I'm thinkin that it's so, you fuckin road whore. Kick stands down. Greetings from road blasted, loose cannon biker bastards and bitches. Eric Josey Whales, Biggin, Johnny Weed and Eric filled our paws with cold devils urine (a.k.a Budweiser/ King of Beers). Then it began. As our friendship and brotherhood quickly developed, this is what I was told hours, days, maybe minutes, and definitely years later by Pokey. Verbatim, she says "Daddy, look at this old school Mutha Fucker rollin in with his apes, his ol'lady has a wicked nice ass!" Our first introduction were furiously smooth, real, cool, mad... H-Wood and Pokey approached from his ape hanger, speed machine and her comforts "o" home conversion van and we went straight at them. H-Wood said "nice iron bro", Spartacus says "nice apes on your horse bro, I'm Spartacus and this is my wicked wife, Rainy." Hollywood says "Pokey, show em your tits, show em your tits Pokey." Pokey says "all right Daddy" and outcome the ta tas, nice tits. All natural, tiny little, raised from the womb biker, whiskey drinkin, dope smoking, pretty girl.

I counter with Rainy, hottie pants "Show em your ass, show em your ass, Rainy." Trophy ass. Rain slithers her heart shaped tight sensual sex crazed backside killer ass outta dem der Levi's. H-Wood and Spartacus drank heavy hammered pulls from the well of mad alcohol and history is made. "Give it to the Biggin, he'll eat it!" was shot out of H-Woods free spirited brain next morning, at whiskey, pancake, staggerin, blues breakfast time. Biggin was running savagely in white boxers and motorcycle boots, support gear and Jack Daniels and then "The Ghost of Elvis (a.k.a The Biggin) stepped into Captain Hollywood's Travelin Freakshow.

I, Spartacus, had become engulfed at "Show em your tits Pokey". H-Wood is a bad, mad, ancient, Choctaw biker Shaman. At the time, although mad and free to the extreme, he was smashing out a livin in the I.B.E.W., for a specialty outfit outta of Beaumont, Texas. H-Wood, Poke, and Rainy were road trippin, away from home Texans (Rain was actually born in Opelousas, Louisiana, makin her a crazy coon ass) but dispossessed Texans just the same. Now as for me, old Mohawk Spartacus, I'd been to Texas several times before I met the wacko Texans, but I hail from the land of the Iroquois. First people. So at AM Jam '05, this group of traveler's ate, drank, and danced. Laughed and sang. Next morning, after ridin back from central stage in the pourin rain, my smolderin wife Rainy and I crawled, laughed drunk into our tent. The Hydraulic Warrior soon smashed his whiskey drunk laughin carcass into camp. Fires were burnin low, the sky was pissin down. He blundered intentionally with mad drunken Czysz humor and psychotic laughter into our tent. Rainy's body heat was volcanic, so of course she was in the middle, Johnny said "Just let me curl up next to your wood stove Spartacus, I'm stoned, soaked drunk and freezin." I said "Coozy up to the woodstove bro", and Rainy's body heat, intense body heat, kept the tent warm.

Next morning, sun almost up, music, explosions, straight drag pipes barkin out a new day, laughter, whiskey... the Hydraulic Warrior seeks whiskey and bacon. Rainy and Spartacus get some passion. The conditions were just right. She sucked my swollen purple cock so fast and great that steam was comin off me and her mouth. Everyone cheered and howled at the spectacle of free spirit maximum pleasure connection. H-Wood and Pokey were makin up some mad biker breakfast burritos, H-Wood was actually overseeing the operation, We partied our fuckin selves loopy all day and on into the night. Excessive consumption to put it mildly. We got so fucked up in the grandstand that for the first time in recorded history, I left my little hard belly, Rainy, in the ladies pisser without an escort, for a few minutes, I'll never forget or live that one down. Until that moment in time I had guarded her with my life, but I suppose with all the pains and affairs she threw in my face up to that point in time, I had a, shall we say, a Pink Floyd "Momentary Lapse of Reason." Oh and by the way which ones Pink? So in a ragged state of rampart biker excess, we said our farewells.

Wearded Beirdos: Myself, Captain Hollywood, and Biggin at JJ Cycles, Wheelersburg, Ohio

We exchanged praises and accolades for the depth of lunacy that was exposed to one and all and Hollywood said "Listen Bro, I'm gonna have a little time off work, so we'll come and spend a few days with y'all." I said "alright den." We, the Hydraulic Warrior, the Biggin, Rochelle, Rainy and Spartacus rolled West. Back to the land of lunacy, that we just came from.

Bout 5 days later, we got the call. It was too heavy to absorb. H-Wood and Pokey were headin to our longhouse. Immediate-

ly, mad preparations began, stock up. Get a bunch of mad scientist substances cause weez entertaining mad Texas bikers.
Lots of good grub, booze and smoke. Some big ol Northern
hospitality. "Biker worthy, smooth style", I says. The two beautiful free souls rolled in both barrels, guns a blazin next day. A
lifelong friendship and brotherhood became chiseled in stone,
Like I stated earlier, this will be a most extensive chapter. It has
been six years since we all crossed paths, but man, we been to
Graceland and the tale must be told, so I'll keep going, hopefully knowing enough to get it all down.

So the Texans roll into Upstate, New York, Welcomed with
open arms, open minds, and hearts cause these Texas bikers,
Hollywood and Pokey, are maximum real, just like their welcoming committee, Spartacus and Rainy. So the interchange
of real unfolds and unravels. Ridin, drinkin, laughin, dancing,
disagreeing, (wenches for the record). Mostly smooth though.
See, these two Texans and two New Yorkers are classic. We
mesh freely. The first weekend lasted 10 days, 10 great hilarious days, The I.B.E.W. Texas hell riding independents say
"duty calls", back to work. Power and chemical plants in N.Y.C,
Pennsylvania, Jersey, and Delaware need to be built. So off
they peeled, as I continued to "black top the world.". The first
visit, I guess the next several, were "iffy at best, sketchy at
most" or vice versa. I'm drinkin and smoking weed all day
tryin to document this chapter. This mad fuckin recollection
of Choctaw, Mohawk paths crossing, throw in a little Mexican,
Cherokee, Welsh, Irish and German. That adds a little heavier
twist to this excursion.

So on to the next visit of many, "Just staying for the weekend"
"As long as we leave by noon" says H-Wood. Hog repairs and
tear downs in the driveway. The mad Choctaw, well versed and
traveled Madman and his raised Pokey from birth by "real bikers shot down in a DEA sting pappy." Pokey's Pappa, I read the
newspaper articles she saved since a little lass with tears in her
eyes. Yellow puppy, yella puppy, yella puppy. Pokey's big heart
weeps. H-Wood brings his son, Zakk, with him. Gotta a gas
powered chopper with a weed eater motor, lad's just 10, "All
hopped up on Dr Pepper and ready to burn. Pokey is whiskey
drunk, tearin down Sheepskin road long side the Ontiahantague on Zakk's chopper. H-Wood and myself sit by the fire
under the open sky, the alcohol, barbiturates and such have a
minute affect on the Shaman, biker Warriors. "This morphine
patch must be defective bro? I still got a crick in my neck."

Stitch rolls in and Hollywood peels off the patch and gives it to Stitch and suggests he "chews on this for a while" Bullets are sublimely, without sayin nothing to no one, thrown into the fire. They explode and we laugh and sit still and jump all at once. .45 cal they is. Embers flyin, holy fuck. We drank all nite. The sun broke on the oaks and cherry's as Zombie blasted at the dawn. Some days later, sometime shortly after noon time, the Texans rolled out.

Spartacus with H-Wood, Austin, Texas

You can't fucking fathom how it spins out from here, more beer, can't see to steer out of the rearview mirror. On it went. H-Wood calls and says "hey bro, got tickets to Audioslave, Seether and 30 Seconds to Mars at Madison Square Garden nite before Halloween, pent house in Jersey to boot, you comin down?" "You and Rain?" "We'll go in deep." Old Spartacus is chompin at the bit and the deal is sealed. We roll down. The Texans take us to backwoods Pennsylvanian Gin Mills and everyone knows 'em. The bars along the Delaware River water shed are loaded with iron horse tramps.

The October sun and wind is brilliant. Getting hammered, stammerin, singin, swingin, and laughin. We head to the penthouse, the broads take way too long to doll up in a drunken sex kitten state. Me and H-Wood laugh and drink, waitin for the t&a to make god damn sure were late for the show. But it was worth the wait, or not.

Then we rolled heavy, goin in deep, the Big Apple, city that just ain't gonna sleep. In a ³/⁴ ton 4X4Chevy with Texas plates, hand guns loaded, temptin fate, "look out!" as he crossed in tight at 80 m.p.h. in heavy city traffic, like the back of his Austin hand. Confident. Knowing. Fearless. Calculated. Sinister. Comical. I hadn't been here since 1978. It was wild to comprehend that just that summer we had lazily drifted in inner tubes down the Salmon River, in my front yard, outside the windows of my longhouse. H-Wood, Poke, Zakk and Spartacus, as Woodstove and Mudflap filmed our river run. Now we were blastin, high speed into the big heavy. The city of no rest. Vixens, hot sex kittens, demons, psycho's, cowboys, axe murderers, rock and rollers, Nazi's, and witches filled the streets.

First stop the Gardens. Concert bound. Right to the stage, on the floor, young punks not a clue as to who they fuckin with. We grizzled bikers were there for the music, man. After the little retards pushed one too many times at the women folk and the Shamans', we threw some back hands, fore arms, and elbows. Nothing to extreme, just makin a point, as we barked out stern warnings to submit and listen to the show. Security rolled in. 10 young boys on 2 mad men. The thugs in charge were keeping order? At a rock and roll show? Laid the youngins down and out and thanked the bikers for exercising composure, to a degree, so we and our t&a enjoyed the rest of the show. The punks had to go. Good concert. Next stop; hogs and heifers. H-Wood parks his 4X4 on the sidewalk sayin "I got Texas plates, they'll think I just don't know any better, come on bro lets go." Joints packed. We get inside and Rainy is so fucking hot that the hottie bar keep gets on the bullhorn yellin "Hey blondie come up here and dance." I hoisted her confidently and proudly up on the bar. The crowd went fuckin wild. She hypnotized N.Y.C. We all lived every god damn breath of this and it was just the beginning of Captain Hollywood's Traveling Freak Show. "GET SOME!"

Hollywood rolled us into Time Square about 3:00 a.m., stopped his rig and said "get out and take a look you crazy country boy." I got in the middle of the endless neon fury and the electricity that blasted thru the night made my beard smell burnt. I raised my face skyward till my neck ached and then the Texan said "Come on bro, let's go"

Next day Rain and I stammered homeward (I just had to get up and mute the idiot box cause the government controlled news media were proselytizing Barrack Hussein Obama state of the union address about buying American made products when the U.S. government has willfully, systematically sold our work to China, Taiwan, Mexico, and everywhere else on the globe to line fat cat pockets. Tangent, I'm pissed, sorry, just speaking truth. Our leaders our fucking us daily, Vote for no one, re-elect no one! Back to the "Freak Show"

We made it back to our longhouse laughing, Then winter was upon us. In August, on the 29th of that year, the Hydraulic Warrior dumped his iron. I was yellow line, he was white line. Whiskey, exhaustion, and weather conditions, along with a mad addictive personality, left him forever damned with a traumatic brain injury.

I tried to save him for the next 5 years to no avail. He's still with us but by just a fraction of his former self. I'll get to that in another chapter or book. Biggin was alive and well and mad as hell with all that life was throwing his way. Ex-wife, wonderful daughter, struggling thru the American dream.

Then... we got this... mad invitation. Join in. Hollywood calls from Newcastle, Delaware. "we gotta make a mad road trip from here to Bowling Green, Kentucky, to Austin, Texas and we require your assistance. The shit was on bro. The Freak Show was going on the road. I got on the blower and talked with the Biggin as to the particulars of what H-Wood had laid out to me, and we were all on the same page. I almost forgot about pickin up a hitch hiker and scaring the bejesus out if his silly ass. Another chapter.

It was mid December 2005 when Biggin, Rainy, and myself got all packed up inside his 1986 Dodge Conversion van and set out to rendezvous with Hollywood and Pokey. The mad plan was to travel in 5 vehicles to H-Wood's next job location, which was Bowling Green, Kentucky, He's lead in a sinister 1970 GTX, flat black, big motored-up, devil's cruiser "The laughing man in the devil's mask".. Pokey had her Ford conversion van loaded up like the Beverly god damn Hill Billys, Rainy was to drive H-Woods ³/⁴ Chevy 4X4, with his Harley Davidson Chopper "Lucille" in the back. Biggin was drivin H-Wood's company truck with a 20 foot flat bed trailer loaded with gang boxes, ladders and materials, and old Spartacus was rolling in Biggin's conversation van. We had the fixins of a helluva road trip on that Freak Show. Kind of like the Gonzo Journalist and his Attorney headed to Vegas! I'm sure you're "catchin" my drift, "pickin up what I'm layin down? Don't ya know?"

H-Wood and his devil's cruiser, 1970 GTX

Now Hollywood is quite the road Warrior and me, myself, have lived and worked all over. He's I.B.E.W., I'm S.M.W.I.A., and Biggin's a trucker so we're used to being on the road. Rainy's a Navy brat and Pokey's was raised by bikers since birth, so we knew this would be a trip to remember. H-Wood and Pokey had good old school biker friends in Ohio and Kentucky. Years later. (Opening scene of the greatest biker movie ever filmed, by Jesus Wept Productions) "I can't discipline myself on this... I must exercise discipline!!!" Blah, blah, blah, yadda, yadda, yadda" Spartacus said. The German said earlier at his longhouse kitchen table that we should consume more dragon piss!!!!)

Transcriber's note: The author tends to ramble off when writing, depending on his current intake of alcohol and narcotics, as well as, his mental state of well being or lunacy, especially in the next

paragraph, so please stick with me... you... the reader, and we'll get back to the traveling freak show. As I too tend to say "what the fuck!?! However, I transcribe as it is written"

Back to JJ's custom cycle in Wheelersburg, Ohio, tri-state area. "Norm", mad motor head!!! Genuine!!! Gifted me the mother of all hats upon our arrival. Moons later poems were written carnally by "the greats" to express the "racooning of the head". Rides his Harley, drinks hopps and barley, thanks Joshua James. Words of my father verbatim, young version of myself. What a trip in time this has proven to be. Listen, listen, laugh, and drink with me. I'm Mohawk, see!?! Back to the Travelin Freakshow of Captain Hollywood. This is ballistic.

So we roll into New Castle, Delaware. H-Wood and Pokey tell me of a friend. Later, they show me pictures of her ass, wicked nice ass, moons after Rainy has her last break down and replaces my, our, life time (decade dance, of love and laughter. Never met Jen's ass, to this day. Shot the shit on the phone couple conversations. Now Rain, on the other hand, I miss her wicked hot sexy bad laughin, dancing, killin, thrillin, head shakin, singin, everyone turns and watches her walk, ways. You all get that? My baby, she's so fine. I have been so deeply in mad passionate love with some of the most god damn pretty girls in the world that I can't help but to write it down. Passion, passion, passion. That's what makes the planets rotate! No one can tell us differently.

So we roll into the outskirts of New Castle, black and white territory, H-Wood meets us at a food chain in the devil's cruiser. It's a "wintery mix" as the yuppie, worldwide meteorologists might say. The GTX had drag racin buckets in it. Biggin ain't that small, yet Hollywood insists a shot gun ride and "The Ghost of Elvis" heartily accepts. I get the conversion van. Like a stunt double we're all drunk and stoned rollin into Delaware, for the first leg of the "Freak Show". Crab cakes, crab cakes, crab cakes. Gotta thin the alcohol. Maybe a shot or two with the cakes though.

So we arrive at their "luxury suite", just makin the boss man rich luxury suite, Good lookin out, though! So we slapped backs and laughed forehead to forehead, and the freak show unfolded, 2-way radios, pissin in empty bottles, hurlin em out windows on interstate highways, just smoking some weed, Jimmy Beam – "The coolerater was jammed with TV dinners and ginger ale." (Bob Seger version) "C'est Levee? Got carried away on "no school" music" thanx Falcone.

So we man-up at the departure, ground-zero site and roll. Laughin so hard we can't see! "The shit is on!" thanx Rondo! Tarantino! Danny Trejo!

The American highway is flat out, twistin, windin, wide, fuckin open to this caravan of loons. We travel at dangerously high speeds. Look back a few sentences at the description of vehicles in this "Captain Hollywood's Travelin Freakshow." So we're pushin the envelope in America. Why the fuck wouldn't we??? "We" is bikers, fueled by reality of self. Laughin, drinkin, ridin, killin... all in our path that isn't real or genuine. What the hell do we know anyway? We run with ourselves and those of like spirit in the wind. We influence every facet and segment of the world society. Our culture is "the big heavy."

2-way radios, spent bottles of devil's urine fly out windows on American cross roads. On thru the night, with great laughter and heavy feminine tension, we roll thru the mountains and land in Ashland, Kentucky, it's late, we're all hammered and exhausted. Radio chatter. Mad women. Hot coon-ass wife runs over my right foot at the gas station. I lash out at ignorance like Pink Floyd's "momentary lapse of reason." We roll to Aaron and Vickie's. Youngin's. Great folks. Ahhhh... the lunacy. We got fucked up to the wee hours of the morning! Next day introductions to grand daddies down the street ensued. Carpenter, cabinet maker, furniture custom building old man.

Then we all made the rounds. Many instructions. Mad bikers. At some point, in the ensuing hours... , or next couple days?! The show started exhilarating at the break neck pace. Vicky, a.k.a Alyssa Milano and Biggin, started in on, some started in on. We were all on a heavy page of individuality. The details (although undisclosed) remain vivid in the author's recollection of said events, ha, ha, ha, fuckin ha! I can't recall the name of the mad confederate hat. Elwood had moonshine, voodoo dope, and we went to mad gin mills all as one.

The next day we roll through Kentucky into Ohio to get stoned with a fine American couple. Now they are in the Western part of Ohio, Buck Brush at JJ's cycle, down home American bikers. They have wicked real hospitality, Couple "o" wood stoves in the hog shop. 60's American muscle cars, wrenchin, long haired motor heads! I got some great flics or is it pics? Pictures and memories. The fuckin Captain Hollywood's Travelin Freakshow rolls into JJ's cycles. You smell the quality of the smoke before it's on fire. So we all speak. We stagger, laugh, drink smoke, and dance round this mad biker realm.

I see an old anvil shrouded with full Mohawk regalia, pick it up and shake off the dust... eyes and mind full of wonder, On my head it goes and I ask the fine American couple "Where the fuck did you get this mother of all hats bro?!?!?!" They says "Friend o mine give it to us in Sturgis years back." "Merry Christmas Spartacus, looks good on ya boy!" (mad chapters on the hat). We're all still standin.

So on into the night we drink and smoke. Old friends and new associates and out comes Kentucky, Ohio, tri-state hospitality and we grub down. Biggin's sleepin in and old Volkswagen van in the back end of the shop insisting that he is "comfort filled"... that's because he is. "That's all he needs" on this road trip, reality. The shop has a couple of a old stoves going. The longhaired country biker and his house mouse get out an air mattress for Rain and me and place it in a cluster of Iron Horses on the cement. Hospitality. Next morning I wake with my hard belly hottie, surrounded by hogs, hog parts, and laugh exclaiming "god damn girl" I musta woke in Valhalla. Odin grinned, Crazy Horse laughed. We were back on the road, on the freak show (side note). On our way we stopped to put hard earned $$$$ in our gas tanks at a filling station in America. Somehow a misunderstanding developed. The stations owners were of an ethnic background, different from ours, and made an inaccurate assumption. I became enraged. I hear and see. A blood bath was diverted after some furious, verbal, mental onslaught facts, laid into these idiots that misjudged bikers.

So... on we trucked. Hollywood and Pokey instigated a wild state of freedom. So Biggin, Spartacus, and Rain rolled headlong into the challenge of being free. Illusions bar; drunk, stoned, retarded, local midget wrestling. Now that's back woods American, Russian, Canadian, entertainment. Promoter says "place your bets, gentlemen and ladies and ladies and gentlemen, place your bets!" So I have never been to this Kentucky gin mill in my life. We place our bets. Listening to the promoter's spiel, we laugh and bet. "First brawl is for "Al Kee Hol". Good fight, they give it their all. Next fight, about a $1/2$ hour later is for a joint. "Place your bets" says the promoter.

Laugh, drink, smoke, and dance. Good fight in the second bout as well. All bare knuckle. Then comes free spirited dancing with fat, seriously ugly girls. But we're just bein real and havin fun. Lil hard belly wife of mine Rain, gets bent on my level of self confidence. Fat chicks sell bad narcotics to Pokey. Hollywood and Biggin stuff fat chick into the car, the devil's cruiser, to take her out I Kentucky darkness for some "brain fever" Thanx David Wilcox. We're all drunk and the locals are buyin crack. I just wanna fuck my hot Eldoon woman, and after bad argumentation, crawl upstairs to the rest of the evening. I hear all their words downstairs. I am a machine. It is pounded in the thick black ink of my forearms by Jimmy Bristol at my kitchen table. Ha, ha, ha, ride.

So where'd we leave off????

Rain and I are tryin to seduce "Alyssa Milano". She's way more proficient than me. We leave the bar in a state of doom, drunk, wacked, and hammered. Not being cocky or self absorbed but I can leave bars in that state. We went to a mom and pop retail beer sale impale place. They knew H-Wood and he knew them. They were happy at his reappearance in the Buckbrush. Conversations of big coal projects ricocheted.

After all that has been, it will be heavy pullin it from my pen. Rain was so infuriated at out high speed journey that she ran over me at our first gas stop in "Kantuckey." We're back at AJ's cycle. Early morning drunk. Frost all over the "70" GTX. Mad ride, on a mad road "You just drank my piss bro" blah, blah, ha, ha. Everybody out there readin this with a biased opinion can fuck off! I know that I leave out a lot of details, my travelin parties can fill in what is left out. Interview them crazy bastards.

I went upstairs around 2 a.m. I heard the crack smoking conversation down in the kitchen, in Kentucky, as I longed for my smolderin hot wife, Rainy, to engulf me and chain me in her hot sexuality, but we just argued with one another when I said "All I want to do is eat your ass... ...... " I seem to bring out the worse? Worst? In my broads. They love all the freedom, humpin, suckin, fuckin, passion, beauty, real, outta the gate. Then they realize that there is no way under the sun that they can fulfill such freedom. Onto the next dumbass sucker they go.

Morning, sun is rising up. We is headed to Austin. Take some pictures standing with flat black devil's cruiser and then we're rollin to Austin, Texas...

Aaron's Place, Ashland, Kentucky... on the "Freak Show"

In the middle of a drunken night bender we roll outta Kentucky headin for Texas. It's closing in on X-Mas. H-Wood and Pokey got family round Lake Travis, the hill country, goin home for an American biker X-Mas, new found, lifelong bros in tow. We roll into Graceland, mutli-autograph signings. Down to two rigs... Biggin's "86" Dodge conversation van and H-Wood's ³/⁴ ton starring "Lucille". We stop in Arkansas on the Northern Texas border. Purchasing knives of the stiletto variety and mosquito traps.

We roll through and Hollywood and Pokey break off to Round Rock, Texas. Biggin, Rainy, and Ol' Spartacus...the shovelhead Shaman, roll into Grapevine. Gotta visit Rainy's mom, Jerry, and her Aunt Mary, sister Cheryl and English Steve. Stereo trouble in the driveway. Upscale Texas. Rainy already divorced me in "03" but it's "05" and we're still lovin each other. We take in the posh environment for onwards and upwards of an hour, then we roll to Round Rock. Blast past Waco, Texas. 86 Conversion Dodge van, we meet in the desert. Pokey's cousin is a lost Jehovah Witness. Good conversation about religious truth and lies ensues. After all, we are only ourselves. I, too, was a lost Jehovah's Witness at one point. Can you fucking imagine such a graphic level of diversity? Bikerman, godman? Back to the Freak Show. Tangent.

Hollywood proclaims "Weez headin to Austin, goin home, co-min in hot, goin in deep. Se we fuckin rampaged in. Local boys and Northerners. Note: I'm sketchy at best, iffy at most, that I can only recollect my version of the "Freak Show of Captain Hollywood" travelin. So I encourage my patriots of the show, to shove their ideas into this book of memory. See, H-Wood is back home seein his "jacked up on Dr Pepper and ready to burn" son Zakk, and Pokey is Texas born and raised, lovin her daddy and we gotta lot of Jimmy Beam and Jack Daniels. The smoke is plenty smooth to boot. Rainy's grandma and grand-dad is buried in Ananac. Old Spartacus hails from the land of the Haudenosaunee. The Iroquois. People of the Longhouse. So we're all dancing.

Hollywood starts us out on 6th street. We walk into every gin mill on the strip. Music, different music, rails from all doorways. Laughter, laid back, open arms hospitality, dance, drink, howl at the moon, welcome to 6th Street, Austin, Texas. Let's go smoke a joint with Stevie Ray's bronze, mad, Roman statue. "All right den!" H-Wood.

Coyote ugly. Rainy dancin on the bar. Encouraged by the bull-horn sportin hottie to "Get up and dance" She hypnotized the live music capital of the world. On down 6th. Metal, blues, folk, jazz, rock, punk, country... welcome to Austin Texas! Thanx. First time of several excursions ha, ha, ha, ha. So we staggered round in your mad Texas town and suddenly we was guzzling booze at the Saxon Pub. Willy Nelson's tour bus from 1969 had weeds, Texas weeds mind you, engulfing the weather baked tires, and I could barely comprehend this H-Wood and Pokey level of heavy real road Warrior. But I know and comprehend-ed, just the same. It was an authentic Texas dance party. Seth Walker and the White Ghost Shivers was smashin the Saxon Pub. (I've written about this briefly in other chapters). I'm cer-tain that this event will rear its ugly head, "Again, and again, and again." "You can bet your ass on that baby" thanx Ted Nugent.

So we're poundin alcohol "Stevie Ray", dancing, dancing in our regalia. Crowds intrigued, insecure rednecks, is getting suspi-cious bout the biker freedom expression. Too fucking bad. You ain't gonna fare well... question the real freedom? Better open your head redneck, fore some sons of bitches smashes it closed.

The lead singer was hot, dressed up like Santa Satan, Patron Saint of Hookers. Ol Seth Walker was 11 feet tall with a plaid suit. Had a Mexican assassin on lead axe. Horn section. You can't possibly accept that I recall all this? Oh yeah, we ordered many drinks and spent our hard earned capital freely and without reservation. Welcoming the strangers amongst us to partake freely in our offerings to the Gods of Consumption. (We got some wicked photographic evidence of the show, it's on my kitchen wall). Right around this point in the tale, Rainy was misunderstood by a limited intelligence beer tender, bar wench and this is where the "Travelin Freakshow" jumped to a whole different mad level!!!!!

After crashing the young shit bird (that struck my hottie after the Jersey remark), over the rail, out the front door, His head hit the gravel hard. Full body weight of mine, smashin his head into the cold December Texas gravel. (There is so much more here).

Now, here we head, to the next tangent of this fuckin Freakshow. 30 pages and nobody's even been arrested yet. (I missed, almost missed the hotel pages, car alarms, etc) It's 3:45 a.m. on 2.3.2011... I'll pick this up in da morning.

We all shared one hotel room, one night on the way down. Two beds so Biggin had to be issued a fold up single. "Show us your poop ring Pokey", H-Wood's giant shit log in the toilet, no paper. I said "How the fuck is that possible?" He says "I took a shower, no sense wasting paper bro. Just poopin in the toilet like a big boy." Then some fuckers car alarm went off at about 3:00 a.m., right outside our window and it kept goin and goin, it was nuts. We (Biggin and myself) went to the front desk and said find the shit bird with tag #blah, blah, blah, now or we're gonna smash that car to a fuckin pulp. The girl finally located the right douche bag (it was a big fuckin hotel) some old fuck who slept like the dead and didn't even hear the fuckin horn blastin for a 1/2 god damn hour. So back to the bar room brawl...

The joint was packed, the band was great and the punches were flying. Hollywood and Biggin were whackin the rednecks pell-mell, Pokey and Rainy were punchin and kickin, throwin drinks and bitchin, I was still pounded the one asshole, when everyone started yellin "The laws comin" "Sheriffs is on their way" "You Bikers better get while the getting's is good."

I said "Come on lets bail" and we all headed across the parking lot to the van. I was out front with the girls, who were right behind me when H-Wood and Biggin decided to slip in the side door real quick and dot some more eyes, Crazy fuckers, Rain and Pokey got in the van and I headed back for my bros when they come runnin out of the front door just a laughin and hollerin "WE GOTS TO GO!". No sooner did we pile in the van (which is loaded with coolers full of beer, half empty bottles, big bottles with the handles on em, Jack and Jim, loaded fire-arms, hammers, ball peens hammers, and good weed) backed up 10 feet and then we're surrounded by Travis County Sher-iff's Department. Blocking our escape. They had a really beat-up lad standin next to them pointing at us. Biggin and Hol-lywood's victim, one of em anyway. They shined their cruiser spotlights in the windshield and H-Wood says "I got this , I'm from here." He was first out and still has a fresh bought stilet-to from Arkansas in his leathers. Needless to say "cuffed and stuffed". Next batter up, Biggin. "Get out of the van big fella" on the bullhorn. Now Biggin forgot that he had brass knuckles that H-Wood gave him for X-Mas, as it was Christmas after all., still in his leathers. (I put mine in my duffle bag cause I wear tons of battle armor right out for all to see). So Biggin's cuffed and stuffed, both for concealed weapons.

Left to Right: H-Wood, Biggin, Spartacus
brawlin at the Saxon Pub, Austin, Texas

Now it's my turn. The public servants of the people of Travis County, Texas didn't know how to take me. The hat, all the spikes and nasty rings. I had a blade on my hip that my great Tacoma brother Sigman "Billy" Wachter (R.I.P) had gifted me, and the Nazi's confiscated it for blade length and handle style. I use my knife as a tool, not a weapon. It's for cutting up blocks of cheese, sticks of pepperoni, pig knuckles and such... but they took it anyway. Don't try and talk to a cop about "sentimental value" at a bar fight. They didn't take anything else, and wouldn't listen to my reasoning on "just let it go, man it's x-mas, we're going home, and the rednecks were the aggressors." Good news is they never even talked to the girls or went near the van. We would have been seriously fucked man. I had no license at the time (DWAI's) just 2 in 28 years of driving under the influence, "just kidding". So they let Pokey drive. She was stoned to the bone, whiskey wild, and wound up like a Texas twister from the brawl. I got in the back and Rain rode shot gun. Pokey couldn't remember where the hotel they booked was at for a while. Lotta drivin around. Biggin and Hollywood were getting their orange overalls at Travis County lock up by now. We found the hotel. What a fuckin shithole. Run by newly landed immigrants from camel country. The bed linens weren't fit for a sick fuckin stray dog, no heat either. It's fuckin x-mas time 2005.

Pokey's on the phone trying to get a bail bondsman and a lawyer. Pour beautiful Rainy is exhausted. She fought hard. I'm pissed that I'm not with my bro's but I'm lookin after the wenches. No concealed weapons on me and the asshole I bashed had no balls to point fingers at me to the law. So I wad up all the bedding and head to the office. I told the little brown men behind the iron barred window to "get me some fucking clean sheets", I wouldn't let my dog piss in that fuckin room cause he might catch something bad."

I was way uglier and intimidating than what I just wrote through, ha, ha, ha! Brought clean stuff back to the ladies and I slept on the floor. Rain and Pokey wanted me to get up in bed just for the body heat, temptin as it was, my bro's were sleepin on a concrete slab and so was I. Men of honor. Brothers in the wind. We only got about 3 hours of sleep and rolled back out to Pokey's cousin's joint in Round Rock to keep on with the freeing of Hollywood and the Biggin. It was about 6:00 a.m. when we got to Round Rock. I should have fuckin mentioned pages back that on the first leg of the journey show, Biggin, that psycho biker bastard, had a mean Biggin sized stomach bug, first 2 days on the road. Shittin and stinkin like a rancid dead scum bucket. Well I got it bout the time the wenches and I hit Round Rock. When Rainy thought I drank H-Wood's piss she slapped me in my face when I tried to kiss her full sensual lips, and when I shit myself after contracting Biggin's gutbug, she laughed but took mercy on my white as a ghost mug.

That sucked, you know it hadn't happened since I was a little gaffer, "shit myself, damn bro" So I got myself cleaned up in Pokey's cousin's 5th wheel bathroom. The girls were eating breakfast and pounding through the yellow pages and blastin away on the cell tryin for a bondsman and a good mouth piece.

Spartacus and Pokey

Mean while Cap'n Hollywood and the Biggin are dolled up in their orange zoot suits at Travis County lock-up. The 2 hooligans can rarely be serious for much longer than a shot and a beer so here's what's goin down on their end, they've told me this mad account thru and thru. They're lookin at each other through the 8 X 8 glass in the doors of the holding pen, across the hall from each other, cutting up and being wackos. Tryin to keep it from heavy. Get some sour milk and stale bologna sandwiches. Laughin, makin trouble with each other. They get brought out in a line of other unfortunate sons of bitches that the jack booted Nazi thugs brought in to harass for kicks. You all the know the pig mentality "zieg hiel" some wet behind the ears kids in line between the mad bikers and H-Wood says to Biggin, "not again, not another one" Biggin replies "Yeah Bro... another one." "Fuck me man." The kid says "another what?". Hollywood says "cavity search boy, you new at this?" Biggin shoots back a disgusted look at the kid and says with a twisted grimace "Third one since we got here." The kid tears up and cries "I'm just in for public intoxication." Biggin and Hollywood say "just kiddin fuck ball, ha, ha, ha."

Now the boys are in front of the Nazi desk sergeant, and ol Biggin says "Pardon me officer, but we were never read our rights." The big, powerful Texas pig laughs and drawls "you watch too much TV, New York boy... Judge'll see y'all in 3 or 4 days, now back in your cages you fuckin monkeys.

Pokey's efforts are relentless on the quest for bail and legal service, she loves her "daddy", Captain Hollywood. Rain and cousin, Scary Lynn, are chewin the fat. I'm as green as a poisoned rat, Stomach death, gripped with the fever. Biggin even calls my brother Evil John in upstate New York with his 1st goddamn fucking phone call, cause it's the only number the big drunken bastard can think of, in an attempt to get info on a hometown lawyer. Pokey's persistence and Hollywood's excellent financial status as an I.B.E.W. top flight spark thrower come through blazin. The shackles of tyranny are broke off. It's a little sketchy at this point, but I think the... wait it just came back. Hey whadda ya want, it was 6 fuckin years ago and I'm drinkin, anyway. H-Wood and Biggin got a cab to an interstate gas station, Rain and Pokey and myself were in Biggin's conversion van. Pokey had H-Wood's 4X4. It was 12.23.2005 at about 5:00 p.m. We all laughed and back slapped, danced around the parking lot with shots and beers, what a fucking bunch of fucking biker trash hooligans.

H-Wood and Pokey were rollin to bowling green. Heat trace job on a chemical plant. Rainy, Biggin, and Spartacus were north bound with the hammer down. Biggin had to keep a promise to his daughter Nikki and be with her for x-mas eve. It's good to spend ancient pagan, Christian tainted celebrations with family and friends don't ya know. Rainy had a promise to her son, Skylar, that would also be kept. She's a good mom. As for old

Spartacus, he's just an instigating Shaman and Hollywood and Pokey, Biggin, Rainy and Spartacus said "see ya on the next Travelin Freakshow." As quick as that with tears in eyes and laughter in bellies we went to our cruisers . H-Wood tossed us $350.00 bones for X-Mas road turkey, gravy, taters, and whiskey. We missed one another before we left the parking lot.

Biggin hadn't slept in bout 48 hours so he climbed his giant frame in the comfort of the back bunk. I didn't have a license so it was decided that beautiful miss ass kicken biker babe, "Rainy Michelle", would chauffeur us to the Arkansas border. Spartacus would run the gauntlet from there. After all, he's been ridin and drivin since he's 10 and a license is just $$$ for the government coffers and a way for the King to track and monitor his slaves.

Rainy, tough as nails, got us to Arkansas in about 3 hours, I took over from there, Biggin hibernated. Rain and I talked and listened to tunes. We were cosmic lover friends. We had logged many, many miles her and I. The Freak Show was headin back to the frozen, desolate waste land of upstate New York. Hollywood and Pokey were sayin farewell to family and friends in Texas and hookin back up with the Ohioans and Kentuckians; Norm, Michelle, Aaron, Vicky and Elwood.

H-Wood on the road during the Travelin Freakshow

We stopped to piss and get rid of empties, gas-up, and get jerky and cheetos, popcorn, peanuts, and such... ha, ha, ha. We still had a bottle of Jack and a bottle of Jim for road companions. I hammered that 86 Dodge van for 22 hours before I started seein shit that weren't there. It was about Pennsylvania when the snow set in. Rain was bushed cause she stayed awake with me the whole fucking time. What a wild child. I woke the sleeping giant. Biggin took over in Northern Pennsylvania, the last three and hours was a hell ride. It snowed like a bastard whore from hell! Lake effect from Syracuse, New York, straight through to the village of Pulaski, New York and our longhouse in Pineville, New York.

It was about 9:00 p.m. x-mas eve when we rolled into home, on the Ontiahantague. The snow on the front deck was tit fucking deep. Fuck me. Welcome to hell. Rain and I exhaustedly unloaded our gear, double time cause Biggin and Rainy had promises to keep. Me and Biggin had a quick shot and a beer. IO Saturnus, Happy Fucking Birthday Jesus, return of the Roman God of the Sun I know, it's just mythology right? Right? Biggin rolled out in the blizzard and Rainy and I did the same. Promises to keep.

The ensuing legality and many return trips, and ongoing adventures of this mad fucking biker entourage will continue to be written. So it has been done, so it will be written. Hope you mad word eaters enjoyed the feast. We'll eat a lot more real soon. It is always a pleasure dining with

you fuckin road whore tramps and hooligans. Later, Spartacus. "I'm off for shots and beers and bongs."

2.14.2011 My valentines are fucking everyone but me! You'll have that. Thank you, good night, blah, blah, blah...

On a side note: Rainy, Biggin, and I went to see our brother Johnny Czysz, a.k.a. Hydraulic Warrior with gifts on X-mas day. He was in Faxton Regional Rehabilitation Center from a tragic motorcycle wreck. It was day 119 for him and we kept in constant phone contact while on the Freakshow. I have asked the German to pull from the "Czysz Journals" (two composition books) and add to the Travlin Freakshow. The journals are a daily log that Rainy, Biggin and myself kept during the Hydraulic Warrior's road to wellness. They covered 5 years of the matter.

Excerpt from the "Czysz Journals" Page 132-135. 12.16-12.25 2005.

Thursday the 15th of December 2005

Hogman called from Vermont to check on Johnny. I called the University Hospital and Dr. Hodges office to get logistics on John's appointment. 464-XXXX

It is just a pre-op evaluation today

Thursday the 15th of December 2005

We got to Dr. Hodges office at 11:20 a.m. and Johnny arrived at 12:40. He was accompanied by a young nurse from Faxton. He looked real good and the first face he saw when he came through the door was me. He smiled big. Rainy, Biggin, and I reassured him everything would be cool. We hung with him until the noon appointment.

Friday the 16th of December 2005

I called to check on Johnny from Delaware and see how he made out. Once again, no one from his so-called "family" showed at his appointment or afterwards. John's nurse told me that he was in good spirits and he told them when he got back from Syracuse that "Dr. Hodges saved my life."

Sunday the 18th of December 2005

Called Johnny from Kentucky. His nurse said he was doing very well and improving every day. Also talked to Dave LaSalle. He has gone to University to try and see Johnny on Friday night. He is very concerned about John.

Thursday the 22nd of December 2005

Called to check on Czyzyman from Texas. Nurse told me he is doing really good.

Saturday the 24th of December 2005

Called to check on J.F.C. I talked to Marylyn and she said she gave Johnny a pair of flame shades and he's been wearing them all day. She said he's doing really good and I told her to let him know that we love and miss him and we'll see him x-mas day.

Sunday the 25th of December 2005

Rainy, Biggin, and I took John some x-mas gifts and stayed for about 5 hours. It was really great to see John. He's still having a lot of difficulty talking. He said "I can't read" and "When I get outta here I'm never coming back." He was in very high spirits, opened his gifts on his own, we laughed and he joked around like he always has. Rainy gave him a nice long massage while Biggin and I went out for a talk. He liked my hat and we took some really great pictures. He was wearing his new shades and flipping us off. Before we were leaving he got himself up, asked for his one sided walker and asked me to take him to the can cause he had to shit. He's wearing his regular skivvies now and is much more able to normally take care of going to the can. I just helped him a bit. We told him all about our road trip and showed him the pictures. We tried a couple times to get a hold of Hollywood and Pokey but were only able to leave a message. They wanted to wish John a Merry X-mas.

Thursday the 29th of December 2005 (Rainy's Birthday)

4 months now. Johnny Czysz called this morning to wish Rain a happy B-Day!!! That was great! We went to see him for 4 hours today. He's making progress every day. He bought Rainy a B-day card from the gift shop and gave it to her as soon as we got there. We went to the cafeteria and had some fries. I put too much salt of them for him though. John asked about getting his tools out of the shop and we told him his "family" already took everything he owns, He's pissed. We talked about riding again and I said it was up to him if he didn't want to ride again and he said "fuck you". He can't wait to ride again. We talked about Jimbo riding again in the spring. He told me to "get outta town and leave Rainy with him". We brought him some homemade basgetti and meat balls and cookies. I also bought him a book about American disasters and we went through all of it and I read to him. Rainy gave him a back massage. He liked it We love Johnny.

- To all interested or concerned, Johnny Czysz a.k.a Hydraulic Warrior is still with us. Unfortunately he will never ride again.

Partying with my dead dad

CHAPTER 9

1.10.2011 My dead pappy's birthday. I am sad and ecstatic that he missed the last nine years. I know he would have laughed like an old wise man. If he could have listened to my Magic Face and Baby Cat, Wacky Cacky, and his Shaman son howl out songs in the morning light. Spider was such an instigator of hound song. I drank to my old man several drinks today. I always do for the start-up day of his singing and dancing, and at the end of his line, singing and dancing, at times we seem to live precariously through each other, I know he would have been amused and appalled, horribly, cynically, drunkenly, responsibly, selflessly and selfishly entertained and likely outraged by the last 9 years of his Shaman's son's magnificently wretched wealth of life's experience.

WW2 Warrior. Earl "Stew" Waterman Jr.

He always said "Life's a quest for knowledge boy", "Keep your eyes and ears open". "Teach and Learn". Happy 85th old man. Say listen Earl, "How's the wind and such meshing with the big dirt nap? If anyone can pull it off simultaneously, tag "you're it". I've been seeing a lot of you as of late. Some good, some not so good... good to see you... regardless. "It's just my dream state" right paw? Or something big sinister?

My pop, how I miss your furrowed, angry brow. You observed with quiet diligence, my family, husband father interchanges with Ili and Cynthia, Rain, and Sky. You counseled me on my successes and failures, wish you could've been here for the Magic Face and Babycat years. You would have been yourself the whole time, that kind of shit goes along way with me old man. You know it always has and always will. Two years after you split I made the old bend in the river my home again, after all the mad time, moons ago. I asked you before you left what I needed to know and you said "you'll know when you know". I still don't fucking know pop. Tomorrow I will see your old faithful bird "Kate" for her 75th, she's tore up on you being gone. 44 years, much respect, those days are no more, ceased with your generation. All I ever wanted, all I'll never have. Maybe I didn't listen fucking closely enough as to what was to be done? I doubt it. I can't say or lay blame on anyone party. I know for a god damn mother fucking surety that I gave every ounce of me till there was nothing left.

My Dad, Honolulu, Hawaii, 1943

So through the mistakes and at the end of the line I'm left with nothing. GET SOME! GETSOME! GET SOME! Buck up, boy. But you lived your life with one wife and four sons and went to the ground knowing that you succeeded and no one took away what you worked your ass off to establish and maintain. Till the last breath. Praises and accolades you old Mohawk Warrior, Welsh tough guy. I used to have a picture of you shaving your grizzled mug. I took it through the old look through the top flash pan brownie camera that you started me on. Your side of your arms were emblazoned with pacific theater black work, skin, Indian red. Somehow my Hungarian gymnast first wife discarded all my old flicks including and not limited to that particular series of lunatic photographic historically imperative important Joel Scott Waterman's visual life's experience. Quit yer bitching, it's got to be getting old.

If I could sit down and write what I encountered hanging out with you, past, long past, and my current state of living with you in recurring dreams and visions it would make for perhaps an interesting and intriguing read. But alas, god damn, holy fuck, son of a bitch, lost and directionless is I.

My Dad... missing the wind

Haunted by dreams, drowning my desperate disillusioned, depressed, dead, danger brain in mass quantities of cheap white man drink. "Budweiser = King of Beers". Been side stepping the fire water for the most part, Not sure how, but that's what's happened this round of me fightin for my silly fargin life. What the fuck is life anyway? Wide open highway, chaos and structure, black top and gravel, dirt and rapids, fidgety and composed, genius and dummy, the ugliest, prettiest bunch of information and bullshit that we get force fed or gobble up hungrily of our own level of consumption. Ha ha ha ha ha ha ha, I'm trying to chew on it and choke it down. Sure is a tasty dish this "life", shits happening here that maybe doesn't happen elsewhere. Sure it does somewhere Iono dog. What a pure soul of mad solid rock and roll, black dog so pretty and genuine. Wow, how can this be? The writing and singing and dancing, pain, torment and romancing? It's all eventually gotta come to some sort of grinding halt or not, what if it does old man? What do you think, Pop?

They all raised their cans in a salute to nothing and everything. "I can't wait to hear the new strings on my bass" Sheldon said as the mad Irish Mohawk Zed kid slid into the kitchen, the twisted mad kitchen and conserved questionably with his ma and pa, Nutela she cried, We played silly focused darts and the score keeping seemed to be relevant. I can't really say cause I'm mad drunk shitfaced. Just rolled into my "Tomb of Doom". Blah, blah, blah, yadda, yadda, yadda, just kidding. Shut up to me! How can this? How can this? How can this? Be? Continue to happen. Yeah! We'll publish this shit. He, he, he ,he, ha, ha, ha, Muthafuckin Ho, Ho.

The shovelhead fired and roared headlong into the dark ugly beautiful night. The wicked young asses in their bad sexy panties devoured the old blues man, his head damn near split in two. Yet, he was just laughing and dancing.

Shot and a beer, shit stain. Can you love? Can you cook? Can you write and read books? What do all of us ever say? Just blah, blah, blah, yadda, yadda, yadda. Well the West coast sons of bitches will beg to differ or maybe concur. All at once I can write everything and everyone and no one will see or listen, or comprehend my writings of the mad human language. What's way better than this? Is a hot, young, tight, mad, bottom rapped tightly around your mouth, lips, nose and tongue just for maximum sexual sensual passionate fun? Get some!

I can't even fucking stand it no more! The shovel head careened into the hideous dark powerful roadway. Whiskey ran down my face. It was dark and light, 22.22 and I rammed myself into herself, please always and never underestimate me, Old Mohawk Spartacus.

My Dad and my Grandma, 1929

If you fuck or attempt to fuck with a mad hard core mutha fucka blah, blah, blah it's all gonna come back and kick us in the blah, blah, blah balls. As to well being and whereabouts I have absolutely no input or concern from Magic Face. Although I repeatedly reach out like a Shaman, no one reaches back. I guess we all live in our mad giant miniscule worlds, right? What's old Mohawk Spartacus know? I don't give a flying fuck about humping some human heartless whore. It's be way better with a spiritual connection now wouldn't it? Fuck off ya Ferrell cats! Can't spell and at this point can't smell my history. Got any miles under your hide? Man I wrote some mad pen shit tonight, Anyone here gonna hear, listen, see, or taste? I got the blues. No ones gonna hear, not today, not tomorrow or yesterday. Ain't none of ya really hearing, none of ya. Perhaps the tough old biker was sadly mistaken on this gamble thought give and take garbage.

I see what I think, I see, I hear what I know what I wanna hear. I feel when I wanna feel. See, hear, feel, no! I love, but I cannot touch. I just saw Doc Hogie looking at me threw the god damn horrible narrow bathroom window. Wheel in his face just passed me by. I winked and said "goodbye, see ya, in the next dream mate." As the Shovelhead headed out to the West coast. "I had to materialize into my own grain of sand" said Rotten. The wind began to blow and the sands began to swirl. I was lost, I was tossed surreal was all lost. I riding the shovelhead headed East to New Orleans and then my ghost that was headed for the East Coast was in my memory so I headed back to the West Coast. I stood on Jimi Hendrix grave and wondered why he wasn't a slave. Now you take it from there... well in my insane opinion somehow I lost me mutherfuckin train of thought. Derailed! Get some!! Same age, never bore children and just wanna live and be free in your own fucking society blah, blah, blah, woof and the Shovelhead moved North.

Alright, for the most of my life I had become oblivious to my arrogance and ignorance... just kidding. Why is it so rough up the chain of command? You mother fuckers are hungry. This ladder of life I broke every rung, and now I'm standing on my big fat tongue. The shovelhead headed North now. I couldn't swallow what I'd seen or how I lived as a human being. There was dust and mud and everything in between, I couldn't believe I was in the limousine. Take it from there "You are a genius Joey you just don't know it." Holy fuck did that just get expressed with the Blues in the evening background? Take it from there! I know you got a great idea of mad shit in your head. "Wow, Neil Young, I'm helping the boy out, yep". Till death do us part, the shovelhead headed South by Southeast. Then a whirlwind sent me into a tail spin as the Blues wailed on into the upstate wasted night. We must act upon our beliefs and not just merely speak of them. I shook my weary head and rode on. Someone else was kissing my girl and my girl is kissing someone else. Damn the bad luck. I miss Babycat. I would've fought till the death, the last breath to prevent any harm to my little friend.

Jim Morrison was railroaded by conservative, right wing, Fascist, American government propaganda and narrow mindedness, no, wait, close mindedness. You can kill all you want just don't do it if you're swearing or naked. Wake up everyone who is hypnotized in political and religious poison seperationalism. It's almost too late, wake the fuck up, open your eye and ear holes. Let your heart and mind feel freely. Learn to breathe, is my mind so unraveled? That I'm me, myself? What the hell was I coming across with? I could have been something.

My Granddad, WW1, 1914, Earl Stewart Waterman.
"Motorcycle messenger, front lines to headquarters"

My Grandma and Granddad Waterman, circa 1925

"I am Spartacus"

CHAPTER 10

The fetid, sweltering, upstate filthy evening, unloaded in all its monstrous, stupid glory. The exhausted pile of trash biker mad man, fuck ball laughed heartily and disgustedly at himself, then woke from troubled and difficult semi sleep patterns and lack of sustenance to find 11:30 a.m. with DT shakes, an old hound dog friend named Cactus and his shovelhead sitting once again, in the pourin rain.

Cloud 9 Tavern, Tacoma, Washington

It was another tough night in the boxing ring of life. It was another tough bender attempting to sort the bullshit of betrayal out his over worked, over taxed, over loaded, mind, heart and spirit. Every song Godsmack produced was smashing through his lungs. Fuck all that deep and sympathetic shit, "off with your head" and then his Iron went headlong and sideways into the pouring torrential rain as the distant glow of a sick neon gin mill beckoned "gear down, step in, shoulder your Iron, there might be hot pussy in here, or at least a grim or hilarious tale to expound amongst the mad dregs and brilliant deviants that almost dare to listen and speak in such places.

He put the kickstand down and pulled his darks off his dirty weathered grinning eye sockets. Didn't matter if it was long past the setting of the sun, didn't matter if some so called higher being neglected to provide him with infallible sight... all that mattered right now was getting out of the monsoon, a "shot and a beer bro". Shake it off, see what's happening. Wrong fucking move.

As soon as his grizzled frame hit the tattered old pine doorway, there she was... thigh high stiletto black patented leather boots, skin tight Levi's, 35, 22, 35, 120 lbs, a fire storm of madness, sensuality, and straight up pain. Lips, hips, and eyes that could conquer the human race. She must have saw me coming for centuries. Serious conversation ensued, or so I found out years down the road was just a conibear trap.

What a dumbass I was to listen to all the pretty promises. Don't get me wrong, many great times were had between me and my little liar, betrayer and I wouldn't change any of them, or none of them, or all of them. But if I perchance I could try it all again with one or two or three of them, I would without reservation chop off my own biker trash Madman head than feel the hideous void of betrayal from one you gave your very carnal soul to and every ounce of energy to solidify a lifetime gig where it didn't matter if you rode into a sick neon gin mill in a god damn monsoon, alone or with each other.

He flopped over again in his fucking mad, alone, semi sleep patterns, scuffed his old hound's ear, took a long pull off some Jimmy Beam at the bedside and came in to it hot and heavy, gearin down in the monsoon rain with that gin mill just off in the distance...

10.8.2010 You don't owe me nothing soldier. Just put a round in the back of my skull, execution style, cause I'm tired of lookin at my ugly old face and I'll trade your loyalty with my shovel head. Deal? "Good trade." Wind in his Hair.

10.18.2010 10:15 p.m. I have a wicked buzz on man! That weed was fucking excellent! I was compelled to stand in the rain! It's always good to "get your beard wet that way." Out of the cosmos having a great time. I was driven by a sudden impulse to drive home fucking hammered and listen to loud Alice in Chains and relax at my long house!! My hound "old Cactus boy" is a worthy companion to say "da least." "I gotta try and find some direction" I says to myself, some, something or other. I'm stoned and it's good. The music is carnal and ancient, West Coast dark heavy energy.

Layne Staley has the voice of the devil. I love great fucking music, sounds that just race and pound so carnally, primal, demonically, Shamanic, brilliant musicians, tapping heavy into the energy, and blasting it out louder and prouder! Mad music! Get some, I have to spend a lot more time listening to music that makes me sing my lungs out. "Heavy music", that I've carried around in my head for ions of time. I'd really be stoned if I was on my iron. "Holy fuck, man!" It is so crazy to me, that I rolled back into this long house again? The last 3 and half to four years have been a great Shaman convention. Many great laughs and wild input and changes have transpired. What wild road! "I will never forget, whatever I can remember", Spartacus. Josh and Cristin are West Coast. Way the fuck out there! Thank you. Wasn't long ago, that on a rain drenched, bone chilling night like this, I'd be riding me "old trouble head", soaked to the bone, laughing at the world through buzz on eye balls! I have to get a camera and film "Heavy partiers." Weekly episodes in our long homes or out on a road trip, at work, just living the way we all do, and just keep filming a "day in the life" type gig, with genuine footage of "Heavy partiers" Just being real. I believe I'd watch that kind of lunacy every week.

It's about 20 past. I got to listenin to the Black Crowes. That's some good, low down, dirty, rock and roll. The snack cupboard starting chanting with the refrigerator, and they "hypnotized me." I quickly conquered the blue corn tortilla chips. And the remainder of my American cheese. I moved on to the Hungarian sausage and xxx cheddar cheese. Getting stoned is a good direction to take. Seems to be a lot of outstanding individuals who take that direction. It opens up creativity. Saltines with extra butter, thank you so much. Thanks Elvis. Reminds me of my younger days when my brothers and me would get stoned and drunk and eat everything we possibly could inhale and our Ma and Pa made sure we had plenty of good grub to eat, damn straight.

I eyed the peanut butter and potatoes with an evil leer, then opened another beer. 11:45 p.m., munchies is over for now. I hate cigarettes and I will kill them. Midnight, overwhelmed by food, alcohol, voodoo dope, music, and tobacco. "Sleep now, I must thank, Yoda." I wandered home through silent streets and fell into a fitful sleep, escape to realms beyond the night, dream can you show me the light? Thanks Geddy. Thank you everybody, good night. The wind gusted up so did the rain and I looked outside and the flag played tricks on my eyes/ Sleep. I did not flee, merely changed the location of me own party. Sleep...

Cremation and Burial with life like ash placement.

The Shovelhead Shaman

"Hideous Gypsy"

"Where ya headed boy?" the grizzled old timer threw out his line at the weathered young Shovelhead Shaman, as he took his brain bucket from his sweating skull and jovially the

Shaman replied "hard to say not knowing for sure... straight to hell I reckon..Greybeard.

I stopped and reflected for a fleeting moment in my overloaded mind, inundated by the road of life that brought me to my arrival at this backwoods gin mill. The smell of good Cajun grub wafted in the fading sun light, as the faint strains of Sonny Boy Williamson drifted through the air. The atmosphere was abruptly broken by three big angry bastards piling out of the front door in a chaos shuffle of shoves, punches and shouting!

The biggest one had the other two in a simultaneous headlocks, dragging their struggling carcasses down the stairs. The Old Timer threw his head back and laughed. I myself was rather amused for I'd seen this scene played out a hundred times over the miles. Then my amusement shifted to furious anger when the youngest one broke loose, pulled a blade, and slashed at the big man, opening his tattooed forearm with a hefty gash and fell backwards into my shovelhead, knocking the old iron to the gravel it rested on.

In a split second flash the grey beard wacked him upside the melon with a telescoping steel rod shouting 'YOU'RE A FUCK-IN PUNK BITCH, JUSTIN". Before the asshole could get to one knee I gave a hard right engineer boot to the other side of his dumb ass head and got on top of him and disintegrated his face with all my furious battle armor, with swift and heavy blows to his beak, pie hole, and eye sockets. The one still in the headlock faired just as poorly. The big man repeatedly shattered his face with relentless uppercuts. "Just another mile on my road" I thought.

The big bastard, who later I learned was named "Hawk" and the Greybeard named "Too Tall" kicked the boys in the ass and told em to "fuck off" and sent em tail "tween" their legs to their rig. "Sorry bout your iron, bro" they said almost simultaneously. I said "No bust, it ain't the first time, probably not the last" as I hoisted old trouble to the kick stand. "Nice gash Hawk, need some whiskey and a rag?". "We'll take care of it inside" he said. "What the hell's your name scrapper? Good beatin you laid into that ignorant fuckball". "I'm Spartacus" I arrogantly, with a sense of faded pride, barked out, "Who are you lads? Shots and beers? Oh Yeah!" I didn't have a fuckin clue at the time that this was the beginning of the end of my last fucking mile of my ions traveled, life long road.

In we went... new acquaintances in an endless stream of years in the wind. I hadn't been to Nevada in many moons, out I figured, as usual it would be a wild good time. I'd never been to this particular watering hole before, outside it looked fairly typical, but steppin through the swinging saloon doors it weren't. The walls were a color I've never seen and the juke box had a steering wheel (thanx David Wilcox). Those were two details that stuck in my brain. Then there was the collection of mad men an smokin hotties that had all gathered inside to get torn up, while their iron horses waited eagerly for the next twist of hell bent energy. Hawk and Tootall ordered up some Jim, Jack and Buds. The bar babe "Leather" was almost too fuckin hot to look at , almost. The smell of the grub made my empty belly growl. Laughs and back slaps were exchanged and then came what seemed like an endless round of introductions. My tortured ancient brain was reeling but I knew I would remember these names and faces for they would be the last ones I ever heard or saw.

The ensuing interchange was to bizarre to depict. The characters almost unique beyond description. Stevie Ray blasted from the steering wheel. As I would come to learn over the next several days, the mad misfits in this broken barroom were transplants from all points in between. The grizzled old Hawk, from Idaho, took me under his wing to make the rounds, as Too Tall busted out a pile of rails and weed and the hooligans all dished out the medicine in their bags, each one as open and generous as the next.

Great deep conversation was everywhere and the music was perfectly loud. The desert sun was fast fadin through the weathered smokey neon windows as a steady drone of Harleys rolled in for another night of hellish lunacy. Another Shaman convention was rollin on, playin out, enlightenin, laughin, dancing, drinkin, livin, the fury unleashed, the knowledge takin in. Another day on the planet of the bikers. Legends, myths and history were again bein made, and at the same millisecond in time..being destroyed.

This atmosphere always made me feel welcomed and at home, at the same time guard up, always leery, suspicious, on the watch, toe the line, look out! You never know what's coming next. Maybe "the forecast calls for pain?" Thanx Robert Cray. "Hard to say not knowing for sure." Old Hawk shouted to me over Godsmack, with another shot and beer. He had a smoldering blond stripper in tow, apparently excited about conversing with the Shovelhead Shaman? "What's your name?" I say. "Rainy... You ever been to Tacoma?" she says. I said "Yeah baby but the "T" is silent." This got the train rollin at high speed with no brakeman. She ran her witchy fingers through my dirty Mohawk. Laughin, smiling, oozing sexuality! She danced for me. Yes another, no not another, I mused my cynical self. Then some other tough mug caught her attention and off she went undulating, writhing, and plying her trade. Oh well, see ya later, or not.

In the hours that followed I met, drank, laughed, spoke and danced with such wackos as Zigman, Biggin, German, Doc, Big Ernie, Cheez, Huggy, Rachet, Hollywood and Pokey, Stitch, Boozer, Stew and Kate, Rotten, Suit, Krazy Cat, Evomaster, Punch, Speed, Six, Skidmore, Debo, Hazard, Magic Face, Eldoon, Maniac, Kitten, Cactus, and Lono just to name a few, But what sticks in my head is when I met the owners of the this mad desert ghost bar. Their names where Jesus and Roxy and they told me the joint was built on a sacred Indian burial ground and the all patrons and guests were ghosts or soon to be. They had painted the walls a color I'd never seen and put the steering wheel on the juke box. We drank a lot of yager and acid during that conversation and at some point in the days I spent their smoked Salvia and high powered hash.

I experienced some mad happenings in that frozen desert gin mill and almost made it out with my hide, almost. I struggled to recall the name of the place as I slipped in and out of scrambled consciousness and black out stupor state. Suddenly as my shovelhead and I careened off the North rim of the Grand Canyon it came to me...The name of that sacred place of loose cannonism, "The Mind"

I woke up on the pool table with two brunettes, a blond, and a redhead blanket. Pushed all off on the floor, through a cheer of howls and accolades I grabbed my leathers, a handful of stale pretzels off the bar, ordered a shot and beer, was informed I hadn't left the bar in six days was offered another paw full of mushrooms by a mutha fucking hologram, slammed the shot, slammed the beer, poked myself in the eye to make sure I was really there, ate the mushrooms, was escorted to the door by trippin ghosts, Jim Morrison and The Doors were blasting out-ta the steering wheel. My shovelhead was on the gravel, right where I left it. So... on I went to the next waiting hallucination. To be continued or not. I had become just another ghost at that desert gin mill.

Austin, Texas 2008

THE JELLO TEST

12.19.2010

Transcribers note: While the author was visiting with a friend, Bernie Kisly, Bernie challenged the author to see if he could truly write off the cuff, as a good writer can. Bernie said to the author **"You have 5 minutes. Time yourself. Write a story about Jello, yep, Jello."**

JELLO

I staggered up and said "Hello Jello" She was all hot, shaky pudding fluff and stuff. Jello's ass was perfect and round. She said she hailed from the Deep South and it was rather obvious by her sexy drawl. We both moved over into the mad section and Jello was glistening, shaking and quivering like fuckin Jell-O man. She slid her cherry ass onto my iron horse and said "ride me fast and hard!" It was then that I realized my five minutes was up.

I'm in the classroom of American Life at the School of Humans.

3.11.2011 "Is this fiction or nonfition??????????

" Howls "Just Nick"...

"Eyes and the Ass"

The Coat and Helmet

CHAPTER 11

I was almost god damn certainly sure that I, me, myself was the "Big Heavy", drifting in and out of a mad ocean of alcohol consumption, blah, blah, blah., my spastic mind was reeling from the events I just plowed through, and I still had the coat on... as I attempted to write this down!! Damn you Cristin Rose how is it possible that you created this mad cloth that envelopes old Spartacus? What were your intentions? Artist? Poet? Singer? Dancer? How did you convince your Shaman, Madman, husband, my brother, my friend, to let me wrap this mad twisted piece of artwork and reality over my broken drunken carcass??? World shaker are yee?!

I was called out of a mad state of drunken whackoism at approximately 8:20 p.m. Took me some effort as my level of consumption was wicked heavy, all god damn day long but, as I figured, there was an attempted rise to the occasion to get fucked up with the younguns! We smoked good weed, and there were mad slide whistles, kazoos, singing, dancing, and I, myself chose to soak it all in. Blah, blah, blah. Just another Shaman evening, always a pleasure though. If just for once I could be you and you could be me then it would be just for once that the mad event transpired. The Coat, the Coat... ...The Spirit, power, energy and mentality that gave the coat to me, myself, Indian Ghost, Spartacus, drunken mad lunatic biker. I retired my festering head to another ice cold can of devil's urine and laughed recklessly at my own shovelhead conduct!

Coat and Helmet by Bird's Eye Bandit

That's it! That's all you get!! Go and get some drinks!!! When the politicians, religionists, and ignorant lizards quit trying to move in on my brain I was able in my furiousness inebriation to make heads or tails of the filthy situation. I continued to try to pin it all on the Coat. Then the fuckin coat said "Hey Spartacus! You mad grizzled old fuckin biker trash bastard! You might want to re-up on cold devils urine you fuckin candy ass has been!" I shot back like a Viking "INAR, or Ragnar, at the mad Technicolor dream coat that was shifting me into its realm.

"Listen... this is ancient", look in the mirror and compare the shapes and colors with the ancient plains Indians, It was at the end of writing this particular sentence that I cracked another brew. The snap of the aluminum tab sent me reeling backwards and headlong into what came next. Holy fuck man, too many thoughts, too many drinks, drugs, ideas, experiences, the Coat was whipping me into a frenzy of freedom ha ha! Somehow or another, I put the shiny old Chrysler into drive and shook all the vagabonds off the trunk, their twisted, writhing, puking frames accelerating into the hot summer tarmac. When I was almost out of range of the twisted broken carnage, almost out of range, mind you, I pulled the metal beast to the side of a nothing roadway, grabbed my forehead, and my swollen nut sack simultaneously and howled into the rearview mirror vainly attempting to catch a last fleeting glimpse of my corneas and retinas, but alas some filthy mythological god took my eye sight. "It's a good thing I had the helmet on!"

I don't know at what point in time I snapped out of the mescaline trip? I was getting a tattoo on my face, it was mad tribal, there was a wicked, hot, young broad that repeatedly told me, almost commanded me, to squeeze her succulent hard bottom as the heavy black ink was rammed into my dirty cheekbones. She assumed that this dirty mad biker would be an easy source of seduction, lies and betrayal. She didn't realize that I was wearing the Fucking Coat, man! Does anyone realize that I'm wearing "The Coat?"

I kick started my iron, let that fuckin evil horse buck, blasted over to see Jimmy and Jimmy and was greeted with whiskey and L.S.D., laughs and howls!!! We were all familiar with our carnal ancient ghosts, somehow riding through a desert, mountain, ocean wasteland of freedom, expression, and reality. I, Spartacus, still engulfed and engaged and engorged in the coat that my sister created, my brother's mad magical wife managed to almost impossibly bring this short story to a potential sequel.

I'm shutting up now and bringing this writing to a grinding, fucking halt. If you got any mother fuckin???? Ask THE COAT. I want to call you brother and sister but it's 2:00 a.m. and that doesn't even matter in my empty realm, but you romancers have yourselves and a son and daughter. So I just throw this mad, sober mescaline reefer, L.S.D., alkeehol bullshit out on this paper, Thank you so much for the mutha fuckin coat!!!!!!!!!!!!!!!!!!!!!!!!!!

Then I dipped my paw into some white corn tortilla chips, obviously laced with heroin and such, no matter how much dip and whiskey salsa I shoved them into wasn't penetrating my thick skull, I took "The Coat" off then and waited with anxiety and apprehension for my execution, Did I eat? Have I spoken with anyone? What time is it? "ayyyyyyyyiieeeee" Who am I? Does anyone really know? After we walked around miles underground how could your little maggot replace my heavy? Madness Girl?

No one will ever understand me. I am alone!! Don't answer, don't call, don't reach out, don't do nothing at all.

I grappled heavy with the conversation interchange. We hadn't spoken in years. Irish he is. I'm still not in love with his exotic daughter, If I'm lucky she won't speak to me on Sunday! I'm so fucking stupid.

Smiling Fox, before I get to the end of the line, know this, I haven't loved you more or most of anyone, but you are truly a pure soul. Thank you for your passion and crossing paths with this raggedy ass lover man. This is the strangest life I've ever known. I could have written so many notes and anguishes, laughs and tears today, as I listened to other artists play their hearts out, pourings of reality and watched dumbfounded as this life passes me by.

A freight train whistle sounded distantly as James Douglas Morrison and Johnny, Robby and Ray rose to mad crescendos in my drunken lost ear holes. I've been replaced, erased and the music of me is close, so close to over. So many deep and brutal emotions I keep inside, the battle scars of attempting to be me and letting everyone else I meet be themselves. The scars of betrayal and deceit. The scars of smiles and comfort, I can't drink, think, sleep or beg enough to rid me of the scars of my life's experience. I write with arrogant vague clarity. I don't give a god damn flying fuck if anyone reads or remembers me, This latest bullshit Christian, Pagan, Heathen Holiday has been by far my loneliest and emptiest.

Loss of purpose, direction and spirit. Blah, blah, fuckin, blah. Shaman? Only in my own head. Let all have breakfast with rapist. My anger cannot be expressed. Lost and alone, outside the realm. Never to see myself again. Hair stands on end. The drone of silence is not my friend, I'd write some more, but my brain is so sore, from the heartless young whores, pummeling with their lore of lies. My heart is broken, my lungs are chokin, my mind is smokin from the flames of brutal ignorance. Empty decadence that I tasted four years of my life in. What a sin? Begin again? Or reach the end? Few understand except the man with the pen.

I've run out of hope, lost the will to live. Given all I had left to give. Goodbye to my family, goodbye to my friends. Goodbye to heartless that brought me to my end. Can't bare the pain of being alone. No one wants to know me or answer the phone. Dialed the wrong number so many times and endless slumber, it's the end of the line. Goodbye Magic Face and Babycat.

Take me far away from the white man's system of lies and deceit, let me dance and sing, the water is in my eyes, the wind in my ears, the earth is my ground, I am lost here as the Mayan calendar comes to a close. It's the end of the trail and I've known this time for centuries as a child. What is happening here? Can others sense it? It's the unfolding...

Of life as we assume, think and believe or perceive, we might know it all but we all of us know fucking nothing and everything all at the same moment in time. Wampanoag, ??????, Cherokee, Choctaw, Ojibwa, Apache, Lakota, Crow, Cheyenne, Blackfoot, Mohawk, Oneida, Onondaga, Chickasaw, Tlingit, Huron, Naraganset, Menomonee, Mohican, Ottawa, Haida, Kickapoo, Seneca, Algonquin, Aztec, Chippewa, Eskimo, Micmac, Nezperc, Osceola, Seminole, how did I even get this far in time in the Ghost Nation and the trading walk? Tlingit, Wyandot, Zapotec, Zuni, Susquehanna, Osage, Navajo, Klamath, Sauk and Fox, Inca, Hopi, Havasupai, Cree and Creeks, Athabasca, Comanche, Kalispell, Shoshoni, Mazatec and my ghost, ancient, tortured, betrayed Indian Ghost attempted to recall the brilliance of this continent in much greater and better times before the singing and dancing and sun, wind, moon, stars, bears, buffalo, wolves, freedom, the very music of life for the first people, was overwhelmed and inundated by the conquerors of European tyranny and so it continues. I re-read this and realize this! I'm movin on. All of a sudden I was transferred into a connoisseur of pretzels and cheese, but I thought nothing of it, because it had happened repeatedly in time.

THE COOZY

For Steven "Stitch" McManus, my friend, my brother. "What the hell is in this fucking Coozy, man? I screamed at myself through a drunken haze as Metallica blasted through the mad sound boxes. Another day of lunacy was rapidly and slovenly unfolding, I had no idea that "it", the coozy, waited in the tall grass where I had ran from it only hours before on a rampage of bearded weirdos mooning unsuspecting by standers on a back country road in the crispy moonlit night. This whole concept of the Banditos coozy was always lost and found as it surrounded my frosty devil's urine. It was at that split mother fucking moment in time that they were upon me. A mad furious struggle ensued and as the pistols, filthy beautiful pistols, unloaded, the coozy, in all its mad glory, stepped into the melee fray, and I had another cold one. Cactus was everywhere. He wouldn't rest or stop singing. The barmaids grew suspicious. I almost had it all figured out... or did I? I was out of beer again... damn the alcohol gods!!! They should never let their prisoners drink go dry, My mind was tornado like, a ricochet bullet so to speak.

The German and the Coozy working on the book... Orchestrator!!!

The coozy bought some Salvia (Dark Matter), no less, and then all hell broke loose. "How's that pigs ear, buddy?" "Pretty

Good". I suppose I was almost actually home. I grew increasingly suspicious of Clancy and his so called love of snacks. Where did I leave my alcohol and glasses? "If you can switch your brain waves over to not give a fuck, it ain't a bad buzz; Stitch 1.4.2011". Get it all out there right now!?! What a lonely tangent I am faced with "write" now! The days without an Iron Horse? "Not good" I say, The spirits that speak with the mad American blue collar observation have been stifled to a mad degree, our ancient level of freedom still exists in our dispossessed modern lunacy, words were exchanged between the mad drunken, ancient "travelers of the mind". "The most distant outpost of the realm" "My mind is just pretty fucked up right now" "I miss my wife and daughter and being accused of being accused of being a pessimist, every time I drink alcohol, I'm totally fucking insane."

"How can I continue to write or speak". My throat cords kicked in by propaganda, politics, left and right and center and obscure experience will tell the tale of your own individual god damn big heavy. The ghosts taunt you, me, nobody, nothing, everything, always and ridiculous, it twists off anger, that's what's gonna come out, good ?????. Cactus can't stop shutting up for a god damn filthy millisecond in propaganda time as all the mellow mad violent individuals said "wow, I'm fucking hammered sorry about your bad luck so hopefully you'll get bailed out by some high $$$ Pulaski Lawyer, you'll always know where to find me Mr. Coozy. The finishing out? What do wanna do? The finishing out? How's does that all go man? Wait one minute. I just asked that? Of my, me, fucking self!

I think, I know, it will fly... but... no one else can make it happen "seppin" for me. Spartacus and friends, The movie, docudrama. "weekly" series??? Take your fat credit card and buy a camera (motion pictures and such) boy!

Against totalitarian Enactments. The dogs I've run with thru "this world" know more about me, perhaps, than the men, women, and "chillins" that I have crossed paths with "hard to say not knowing fur shur?" Russell Scott Warren.

I like eating potato chips when I'm hammered, potato chips is a hell of an invention, the way I see it anyway. Pretend that modern civilization doesn't exist. Go back to your primal and your carnal. No artificial light. Just smoke and fire, sun, wind, moon, stars, earth, eternal, the big, the powerful, beautiful machine, Earth eternal. Open your ear, eye and nose holes! Earth eternal. Eat, sleep, love, laugh, dance, drink, dream, work. Run, ride, tear off your very own hide, yet live! The ghosts all know. Remember what you have seen, because everything forgotten, returns to the circling winds.

I can sing and dance again
Because the loss of lady friends
Has seemed to finally reach it's end,
My friend? Laugh and drink and howl again
Like I used to do!

Almost think and feel today... ?
Driving away, Black, dark
September, Sun rays
Long heavy conversation with the ghost of my father
Where's it go from here?
Have you seen it? Felt it? Touched it? Tasted it?
Kissed it? Laughed with it? Rode it? Wrecked it?
Thought it? Lost it?
Enough, he laughed!!!

Stumblin in the neon grove
Thanks... Mr Mojo Rising
Flags are flyin, Kids are dying
For some fat cat's oil
My blood will boil, Enough to choke
Us out! No doubt, give me a shout
When you get to the other side...

Tonight I rolled a joint from my two year old outdoor and I ain't done that in 33 years! I'm a monster. Just on the odd occasion, when I might be drinkin or thinkin, feelin, ridin, rollin, fuckin, realin. I'm Spartacus, out!

• Nickman a.k.a "Just Nick" says "all this
  shit would make great songs!"

You have no heart
You have no love
Indestructible
Forever lonely
Fuck em all
Deceit and shame
Endless games

You want kindness
Fuck you!

Stab my back
Wrench my heart
Tear my fucking life apart
Fuck em all!
Cold, intense, put up walls
In self defense
Stay away from me
You caused my eyes to cease to see
Fuck you!

Is this my fate?
Is this what you wanted?
I'll move on, undaunted
Mad heart of stone
Torn to the bone
Fuck em all!

Once again, broken, smashed
Mind, heart, emotions, trashed
To the whippin post, forever lashed
Once again...

Once again, hopes are dashed
Love, dreams, devotion, bashed.
My life before my eyes has flashed
Once again

Why must all of this pain be?
When will my eyes ever see?
That love, then lies, are killing me
Once again...

All alone, the road ahead
Without passion, I'll be dead
My old friend Madness, has mislead
Once again...

I don't want your free divorce
I can't ride my Iron Horse
Won't succumb to this evil force
Once again...

Who the fuck are you? Blind old man?
Write that down
Breakfast in "Da Moanin"
Why? "Soy tant lee"
Have mercy
Breathe

Don't get me wrong Cactus, I just want you to be comfortable. Now in the winter of your life, make yourself at home. You'll be 94 of your years, this snow, and you might, ought to be able to relax by now, without my inferior, arrogant, supposed super race, givin ya a hard time about dog conduct.

Pretty young women, Crazy old bikers
Send me your beers, Grindin your gears
Friends, Romans, Country Fed Motha Fuckin Men
Set aside your fears, Cause we're only hear (here)
Till the Dark Rift, shift, drift, and die
Sleep...
The show is only playing on your screen now
Fuck Ball

Author's Note: 3.11.2011 The following is the first time I wrote with a "computer" all in caps. The German told me I was "yelling". I betrayed "pen and paper" Never used the black box before. It didn't last long. Just this page, didn't feel right. It was funny though.

I am writing hammered. I am. I am Viking. I am Mohawk. I am Biker. I am man, no heart to feel, no heart to touch, no breath in my lungs taken too much piss off no gods. How can life cost so much? Blues... whiskey... you wanna get some pain? I dare you to belly up to the bar boy if you think you're up for the god damn mthhafuckin task. Return. I leave punctuation. Darkness encompasses who are the focused entities who are the stoners.

I am smoke signals, can't figure out this black box out. Too much modern for this ol'boy, easier to bring paper and ink into this transaction. Piss off Spartacus. Hey Jesus, fat Jesus, don't ever couch your words with Mohawk me. British hair bags, bearded weirdoes; voodoo dope. Pain, loss, tell you about freedom pictures of life unfolding death, unwinding, can you handle it? Shift????????? Drift and Die. Apes, wind, cabin fever, hot wet naughty drippin cunts. Battleaxe to your face you stupid Sons O Bitches... ...You want passion???? You're better off with the blues. Keep your goddamn guard up Warrior. There ain't room for nothing anymore. No distractions jerkoff puissant... you spent 30 wasted years of your sorry existence attempin to appease the whims of femininity... stop waitin your mutthafuckin time shitbird!

It ain't gonna fuckin happen. The snow melted, the shovelhead roared. Let this be the end of the House of Spartacus, man... strength and honor. German!!???!!!!??? Orchestrator!!!!

- "Wanna get a wet ass?, Looks like rain" Just Nick 3.11.2011

Have you ever in your carnal soul felt the absolute desire to extinguish the minuscule life of a transgressor that should not have ever breathed in the first place???? Betrayal... Betrayal... Betrayal... Betrayal... yeah... thanx Hetfield.

Two, Too Twisted Tangents

CHAPTER 12

2.9.2011 Killing, Rampant killing, for god and country? Mass murder in the name of your simple minded religious deities? When, tell me when, are you stupid ignorant, cocksuckers gonna wake the fuck up? Anyone who believes and participates in such idiocy should do us all a favor and just cease to breath. Laughter is so much more than sorrow. Passion is way better than grief. If we could all just get this down. Return to the wind, the sun, the moon, and the stars.

Got a jury duty notice in the mail today. Now generally in the past I just throw that shit away, no belief in the white man's way I'll pass a talking feather night and day. But seeing as how I'm writin a book perhaps I'll rise to the blah, blah, blah occasion wait is mandatory? Will I be threatened by the king if I choose non-compliance? Don't threaten me with a good time. If I don't respond to the king's mandate of mindless servitude I could be brought up on charges? Fuck them son's o bitches. I've never responded in the past but hey maybe now is a good time to respond? Callin for 30" of snow tonight, ha ha ha.

For they're threatening in "Fury cution" in the United States of America. You may allow another person to assist each time the service is accessed including the entry of the pin. "You will be held accountable and maybe subject to penalties." FUCK YOU! "I AM SPARTACUS" Mother fuckin hats off to the likes of George Carlin, Mitch Hedburg, Joe Rogan and Eddie Izzard... these sons o bitches could make a blind, deaf, mute laugh like one who flew over the cuckoo's nest. I'm so hammered gotta get some shut eye, stir fry, What ya been doin since you stopped shovelin 3 feet of lake effect snow storm pain? Well, I fell sleepily into the next forecast of rampart doom, The phone rang repeatedly. Why is everyone seeking me out? Not Mad-

ness, she never calls she is a deviant that fed and feeds me
dirt, I love her smile, and she has a sumptuous bottom but
her and her ma and pa are dirty and it doesn't seem to matter to them who gets caught in the cross fire. Gotta be world
renowned, This must happen or I am doomed.

E's and N's everything and nothing, enough's Enough, now.
Can't let this pass by. I got up from attempting to sleep I write
without my spectacles. I'm out of tapes, I'm drunk, I'm in pain, I
am alone. I want a beautiful woman to be my lover friend. Alone
am I. I miss my Little Magic Face, Miss Rainy Eldoon, Miss Julie
Smiling Fox, Miss Ili Mouse. I miss being loved and respected.

This session of writing starts hard... my spirit is kicked. My
very best interest will be served by honing in on the heavily
focused level of my ancient friend, German. I can barely comprehend what transpired today, wait a minute, let me get my
leathers off. I'm home.

Solid interchange with my brother, German. Stand point or pe-
rimeter, or tail gunner. You'll get it. All you have to do is open
your fucking ear holes. Some cats I've known recently, are less
of integral fortitude. I am wrong, I misunderstood. I stand true.
I am me, myself, never you. You are you, never me. Takes actual
Ancient's for empathy... go back a few pages... "Let's all have
breakfast with rapists"... ? Has anyone gotten back to that page
in this shitty, dirty piece of goddamn, fucked up recorded history??? It's just pages in front of this page. Trust me??!!??? I
like bone marrow on toast. Tis a fine Hungarian breakfast food.

The fuckin scumbag deceiver and his empty whore grandma
caught bribes on the bay of the ice (Names deleted to protect
the reputation of wastes of skin) Lets go with them and have a
plastic time. This incident, is the last. Hope that first orchestration was a forming of brotherhood... the second orchestration
is the forging of an empire. Tonight I have seen and heard...
perhaps I miss read my friends? This question has arisen fre-
quently throughout the path of time 4 + years of path crossing
upon the start of the German's orchestration . Let attempted
rape go by for the sake of their face, name and business????

Try to pick up where I left off. Just let go. It would be wicked
cool if all the random thoughts that explode secretly, unbe-
known to ourselves and all surrounding us, could just become
a mad cosmic blast into individuality. Smoke some weed. Got

a wooden box full of it on the kitchen table. A bearded weirdo bass player is the owner of the box. He call's, I answer-we, or perhaps I am hammered. Got the blues. Just listenin to the fuckin blues, man. So on with the writings, off on a tangent thought process that, slammed me into high gear in my head it all is. I suspect that my thoughts, though they flow freely, will never and have already emptied me????

Just kiddin muthafuckers. I got da blues baby. If we all give reality a solid, deep, shot... what a silly fuckin shitbird to think this. Sing, play guitar, dance, kill, die, sigh, fry, in an electrical chair, gladiators... begin. Just breathe barbarian. Write what catches your carnal soul. Go on a writing frenzy. Fear and Loa... Hunter. Thank s for your input. Gonzo; Jesus.

A mad hot night, girls were everywhere. Not just any girls mind you. But, all the same girls. Off on a mad tangent I go, on... girls. "I" known lots of em, met good, met bad, met those "straight from hell"/ See shop door for Doom Mood, 2006. Cristus and Sheldonicus are coming to retrieve, left here boxes of weed. Laugh O. yeah! Mad out pouring when I see your smiling face I see no more. The weather needs to break, brake, break, break on thru, must ride soon. Cabin fever ways heavy on me mut-tha fuckin mind. Must ride Apes, winds, hammered, defying, no compliance. (As long as you got some stout actions). Lis-tenin to Paul Butterfield Blues Band, "Born in Chicago". Ol' boy named Geoffrey Delaney, turned me onto this crazy blues band. It was Willow dale, Ontario, Canada, when I first met "Jeff, Geoff" He lit my head up. Genuinely deep and intelligent. "Send in the hemonizer." Fucker could sell Genocide. He intro-duced me to Canadian culture, You know, the music, industry, films, first and foremost, writings, White Horse, Yukon territo-ries, 100 Mile House, you got pretty local girls. Last time thru... 1992. Thanx for the hospitality.

It was a mad year, melancholy fall, record hard winter 92-93, Upstate, NY. We tough this shit out, like all the other American tough guys and goiles, thanx Popeye. No disrespect sisters in the wind on heavy iron beasts. Express yourself. Unique, insane, focused brilliant, brutal, carnal, comical. Pay attention. Be human. Clocks tickin, finger lickin, slitten bitchen twitch, freakin, fuckin, good, bad, best I've ever had. I feel a strong possibility, annihilation, of the dwellers on this planet might come to face blah, blah, blah, yadda, yadda, yadda. Did I spell that in any previous ranting???? We might want to exploit this.

This may continue... dark and ugly. I just had some mad wicked thoughts and expressions, whilst I was pissin mass quantities of devil's urine from my over taxed American level of consumption to mask the suppression of anger... Sound familiar???? Rise up, revolt the heritage of this stolen continent is based on such conduct. Break from non-complacency, push away your apathy, embrace integrity and strength of cause.

Prepare yourselves, open your ears, open your eyes, breathe in deeply, touch it, taste it. For if you don't now, it will never happen again in the stream of time. Those of belief, that "life is short" "You can only go around once." Well speaking from multi hemispheres and lines of longitude and latitude, I'm figuring they're might be some sort of style. NOTE: Let's put this down like a Ukrainian, Canadian blues master you know... David Wilcox, master bluesman, practicing his craft.

Where's it begin? End? My friend... alright. Now where was me. One of the atrocity's I find most hard to fathom is, lack of ear holes, hence a level of listening, understanding, when I am confronted with a caliber level of an individual's personality traits , I get pissed an tangentized. If I knew any better, I'd damn sure know better. Listen, book reader, when this comes out you'll have less than 18 moons, Earth time, to read it, Have a great fuckin time. So I write. If I could get all of it out... if I could get all of it out. For I am mad. Son of Earl, Son of Catherine. Is everybody ready???? Centuries fly by like seconds. What? What? You can't possibly expect me to believe that you think such thoughts? I wish (careful what you wish) says Hetfield.

"It will be a great task." earlier in the afternoon the German says to Spartacus. I'm flippin into an additional page of pages. Perhaps if I had the sensual pleasant distraction of devious cunt, I would be distracted of cause and purpose. "Johnny Lang", "Breakin me" "Wander this World" music of the giants. Pull me into love. Why don't my girls understand?

Which one of us stands alone? All of us born alone, die alone... got twins or numbers over that??? Then that's heavies matters for you and your kin, duplicates, triplicates, son and so on. Payin nothin' come one, mad Canadians. By far some of the very best lunatics that this "so called American" has shared life with. You all know who you are and who I'm referring too. I was talkin to Carmen outta Victoria, British Columbia, this afternoon. I loved the years I spent in "Beautiful British Colombia".

When I built my log home project that my wife Ili and I offered was met with great positive energy by Ed.

This has been a gigantic return road for me. "The German" heavily focused mind you, "The German" throws his fierce reality into the second orchestration. I had to turn pages back to attempt to pick up something. No pick up was made in my turning pages back. What kind of conversational tangent should, what, what are you fuckin with my mind??? What, what converse being? Ourselves? I get conflicting. "Cactus shut the fuck up!"

Now listen, when you're pissin into the "terlit of despair" you gotta be serious mang! Nobody is gonna write this crazy stupid shit. How can this be pulled off successfully? What the fuck man. Seek council with the German, We just got off the phone... uncanny. Whiskey, whiskey, uncanny whiskey, whiskey. How many wolves have you shared meals with? Tucson, Santa Fe, Los Angeles, Vegas, Bangor Biker Bastards, I heard of this cat one time. He moved home from the "West is the Best" frontier... ride 12 months a year. In the frozen wasteland of the Haudenosaunee. Not much deterred the Indian Ghost, Shaman Warrior, for no matter what the course of mad ugly American history, you will and most not detour a Shaman. Look to the sky, We are very close. I like the way that some of the spirits cast us about. How much depth do we have as ourselves ? Asking for ions. Skew, you brought a fucking laptop computer????? Where from here lad?

Are you fucking kiddin me. Stay away from that black silly box machine lad. You wrote earlier of such. How can this be? Whiskey. I'll bet at some point in spherical time, some got it all. Blow heads will be in just that same space and time I just wrote about. Hearty ha, ha, ha, you all might want to contemplate, contemplate and reflect on each other's thoughts, words and ideas.

3.2.2011 Conference call. Friesen Press. Carmen. I better get prepared. Writing spree, shut up to me, blues is free, ha, ha, ha, hay, hay, hay, hee, hee, hee, biker, I must be disintegrated by this, come on.

If by chance
I learn to dance
Ain't no one understands
My mad romance

Stay the hand of understanding

I laugh like mad hellions
Filled with rebellion
Bones of me skeleton
Sounds so insane

Understanding stands, misunderstood once again
It's gotta come from the dawn of the land
Arrogant man, with destruction plans
Would not passion suit you better?
Your words are unread letters

Fear to send
Will defend, reality

So where's this go from here? Words and thoughts set me off!
On a regular basis, I, Spartacus have several, multiple conversations, thoughts, and ideas coming in at me from my compa-
triots, yet some of them, don't actually listen to my ranting as
I come across the same god damn, mutherfuckin way to them.
Whiskey, Spartacus? Yes Joel, I probably ought to be troubled
in no way shape or form, by the madmen and madwomen who
I cross path s with. Sounds like straight drags and ape hangers,
blah, blah, blah, whiskey, dope, gin, blah.

Hah! Ever been on a biker whiskey run? Always mad fun you
sons O bitches. Drink, do narcotics, fight, ride, remember your
heritage and the tough mud and iron and blood and self that
makes your tale of lunacy necessary to be heard by the masses... rise up heavy with your mad story of self.

Never let the powers that be stifle (Archie to Edith Bunker)
your expression... love your lyin whore mamma. Bringers of
ruin to a house of honor. Back to the first page. Man of fierce
honor. No transgression against myself and my house, will be
forgotten. What are your intentions? I feel that I have written
or at least entertained such mighty thoughts as these. Now,
Jack Daniels is at my right hand, Budweiser at me left. No
fucking way I could have posted into a computer this cleanly!

So next page. "Soylent? Green is made out of people"... Heston's writers?

In the early morning sleeplessness, I stepped into a tangent world. Familiar and foreign. Dreams. (not visions) merely dreams. Cabin fever, not good, unaccustomed? Ride year round, buckin drifts, sleds on the bank, at the bar. You're fuckin crazy man. No, just out for wind and shots and beers. You fuckers are sled heads, who really is crazy here? Recall me, remember me, receive me, reject me, in the way that proves to be most comfortable with you, yourself. Just remember... always in the presence, my father's Indian Ghost... book. So unload some page, shitbird.

Does anyone really know who anyone else really is? Stand down Spartacus, go back. Share your lunch with a Grey old wolf on the side of Highway 33, rollin Northeast off the benches of Rutland, past the Red Rooster. All the valley dwellers knew for a certainty who the mountain men were rollin down from Joe Riche, Kettle River Valley. Onto Arizona, Oregon, Nevada, and New Mexico. Four corners Anasazi, Ship Rock, Peyote, military jet maneuvers disturbing my sleep two nights. Check back pages or two. I write from life!

Almost didn't get this date on page. I hope they have a nice day tomorrow. I imagine that the interchange and the conflagration will be a sensation in the poser nation. Now say "iffin" someone drunk, coked, stoned, stupid, ignorant... attempted to rape my spoken for wife, heads were mashed, council with so-called family was sought, not received. This has all, I believe, been made completely and irrevocably clear by Spartacus.

Still (I somehow spelled "Still... Stiff") it has been a twofold orchestrated process. One of the two folds I am well aware of this. My old friend, German, HAS NOT EVEN ONCE DISRESPECTED ME! I'm closing my pen. 2.28.2011, 9:40 p.m.

"Have a nice time. Don't jeopardize paid rent for freedom."

How far can thoughts, realizations and observations of one Indian Ghost can go? I only been this for centuries... funny and not so fuckin funny... just the same, you're bound to laugh and perhaps smile at the familiar. Shovels and Pans and Knuckles and Flats... apes and drags and blood and dirt. Were but mad maximum monsters and reality. Shots and beers... tits and ass...

blues, as Delbert McClinton sings... better off with the blues. I have smashed over, up and down a wicked road. Sure you fuckers can all relate in a way, shape or god damn form. Who is this God you speak off???? So, write something "impotent down!?" Hey German, Spartacus just slammed out 12 pages of thoughts, I will speak to you momentarily of these pages of expounded thought. This is only smooth for the ancients.

When you go with the fake empty cocksuckin maggot not bout nothing bullshit cash man fuck. Tell'm my fists have a pressin engagement with his sorry lyin, worthless head. Stop dancing round with no conviction. What the fuckin bad luck and trouble, gotta kick it to ride it. Sellouts. My life has been so adversely influenced by sell outs. Tired, tired, tired am I. Who's gonna benefit me the most at the expense of my very self??? No one can benefit me enough to compensate for freedom. So here it is written. All hail to blah, blah, blah and yadda, yadda, yadda. I close page now.

The blues music belting into my ear holes subdues thoughts of empty dealings. In everyone's best interest's, for family is involved, I, me, meself is not of the family in question and when it all transpires, I will be "somewhere out on the rim of the broken wheel." Thanx Bruce Cockburn! You have "tough word" (initiated) came up with it though. You ought to hear the music and taste the whiskey. If you hit the bong just right you'll get a wicked heavy buzz on and write about things that might come out of the depths of a good bong full of Thai stick. Got a Wednesday conference call, 11:00 a.m. PST, 2:00 p.m. EST. It's improbable and virtually impossible the author made it this far. End of pen.

New pen. So fuckin what you got a new pen, shitbird??? I'm illiterate, mute, blind, deaf and the man who is writing these garbage thoughts is undoubtedly dumb. Just kiddin, mothers. I never wrote one word of this song, trust me. Just kiddin with all this shit! Celeryously... Got any smoke??? Now come on... how freakin much can you take. So the pretentious stoners don't get remote compliance from Ol' Spartacus for left behind dope delivery. I been subject to playin this mad game "afore" they drew first breath. Show me some fuckin respect or go on with an abandon ship. You cannot spend time with a scumbag that denies defending his own against rapists.

I am cut from different cloth. No leather tells me otherwise. I have over extended my welcome and will leave with hopes of the reparation of your family unit. Blah, fuckin, blah (sarcasm). I tread lightly with the outpouring of the pen in my filthy hand, from my dirty brain, "Couching of words" what the fuck is a "couch"???" Speak your mind Shaman, Warrior, Noble Man, Gladiator?...speak your mind. Mince no words., sugar coat nothing. You wanna fuck??? Wanna fight??? Wanna hold a blind man's light???? Better you just go home and sellin yourself out lad! Ain't been beheld in the throes of a "wenches passion?" in nigh on 8 $^{1/2}$ moons. Better than 8 $^{1/2}$ minutes, seconds, weeks, breaths, years, of bent and twisted subjugation of a species that will never be understood, but always sought after by my species.. Never again by me but eternally by my species. Translate please... comment if you will. Listen, without interpretation if you dare. Whiskey and weed. Blues if you will... on a frenzy.

Why don't you sit down, open your instrument, and play? So David Sanborn and Sam Moore belted out blues in the Mohawk biker bastard ballroom. So what is everyone thinkin, hearin, breathin, and feelin? Out on a night time brutality tangent. You got a throttle in your hand and a kick start on your leg tonight?

Can we fit this in by the Wednesday publishing conference mother fuckin call? It would be astounding to get paid and published merely for being oneself. Now this is the good shit. When the flow happens. Brought on by anger, disappointment, happiness, fulfillment, disillusioned bitter frustration, mad whiskey reefer buzz on, salvia, mescaline heritage, bloodlines, right place at the wrong time, what else may have you, and you may have...

Don't fuck with me, I'm writin and listenin to the blues baby. I got awakened to what I already realized, though in a state of unreal. Makes it more clear. Perhaps. I am unreal???? Highly unlikely, given the evidence and extenuating circumstances? Just checkin, lemme me know furshure, wait. Wouldn't it be better and more pure in form if no betrayal of pen and paper transpired???

See, now I want every word on these pages read carefully, calculatedly, when my Mohawk father and I disrespected each other, then we wouldn't take meals at the same table, in the house of Waterman, my father, when shit got really heavy, we would exchange punches, men of honor, till death. My father, if confronted, with a potential rape of his daughter, he had none (4 sons) but on the event that he did, would have beheaded the son of bitch. Hence I would never have to Ice fish with a cock sucking pile of worthless garbage, My father proved himself a man, I hope my old liars don't cross paths with me. For they will not farewell in the crossing. 4 years I gave honor to their daughter, house and name, my reward is pissed on betrayal by people of low or no character.

Inbreds, decadent, disease, spreaders, I long for a face to face conversation with these empty scumbags. Their consciences so tarnished that they can't look me in the eye. Straight in the eye. Bunch a "fuckin" inbreds, illiterate out of state hillbillies. Nothin against hillbillies mind you, for I, me, myself, is just a New York hillbilly. Difference is, I'm real. They is fake from dusk till dawn, fake lying, deceiving, cocksuckers. Only reason you ain't been beheaded is my little friend... other than that... fuck you lowlifes. If it weren't for rage and adrenalin I wouldn't be breathing right now. See, you can't get this unless it is original manuscript with a sound track.

So are we goin back to the desert, or the mountains before the Dark Rift closes all chapter???? Where ya goin Jim... If you get a chance send in a stunt double for Spartacus... unfuckin real.

You have got to be joshin me. It'd be like going to dinner with Rainy's ex. You have got to be fuckin joshin me, man? You hear that old 70's expression?? Ever? After what we all know? What you been through? Before I ever enter the realm? 4 years since and I stand as a Warrior, as a gladiator. Listen... you cats have a long standin family obligation to save yours and their faces way before I was laid to waste and destroyed by a wenches poisonous lies. Come on. They sign that long house over to you yet? Have you not proven yourself worthy? Again, again, and again? What do I know? What do I see? What do I hear? Happy trails to you, I wash my hands. Tell them all that Spartacus says "Damn you!" and give my love and respect to the innocent. Let's all go have breakfast with rapists. Go back a few chapters.

Ya see, I actually genuinely love my mom, cause my mom has character strength and spirit and conviction. Some other mothers, on the other hand, are lying, drunken, stupid, fake, deceitful, scumbag, whore. Nothin but plastic dirt, just like the scum fucks they runs with for dumb gotten $$$. Those fuckers are virtually illiterate. But wealth goes to "republican Catholics"? Best thing that could happen to them and everyone they've poisoned is fire and slow death. Did I just "express such thoughts?" kids?

It'd be funny big time iffin you all had the stomach for such thoughts and ideas. I won't know sooner or later. I step off and stay away as to not cause further rifts in your "family". No one calls, anymore. I know for a certainty, where my honor stands. Where does your honor stand? I, Spartacus, this is not my name. I Smoke Signals, question heavily, where stands your honor? This matter of question is not light. (Phone conversation, virtually) "Yeah... morning brother... listen tell your ol lady that me, Disrespect and Darkness are goin out for breakfast this morning, I figure I can embarrass him with a few more punches in the face. When you, Smelly and the Bass Man, get in, call me so I can kill three turds with one bone. You have no idea how your lack of actions and integrity cuts me. Won't be the first one to dissolve this so-called brotherhood, so, in as how you cats can get back to the business of sell out prisonership. Did I hear any of this right, before I made the decision to bail form your longhouse?"

I am thoroughly disturbed, but hey, sucks to be me, a man of integrity. Listen, do us all a favor and count me the fuck out of any and all future transactions. I know what I just heard this evening. I am on a different page from you two. I hope it all comes round good for ya, old friends. See ya on the other side.

The piano railed on. I don't have any tobacco. I have whiskey though, Cold Satan piss too. Little bit of Bonnie Raitt to fill my empty void of a pretty, beautiful, psycho wench, caressin my nights, answered by Austin's finest. "Stevie Ray Vaughn, mother fucks!" why must those, some of those, who claim alliance, continue to impale me???? Fuck off Spartacus, this is not my name. Make sure you run the gauntlet of law enforcement to retrieve 3 bucks worth of weed in a sentimental wooden box. Maybe you can burn a bowl with the Damned on the ice tomorrow morning? I'd participate, but I have an appointment with reality in the morning. Apologies, maybe them cocks could ply my sensibility with trade goods, unlikely. None of it ever set well with me. Nice thought, I'll hold my own. I should not let this long known conduct disturb me so deeply, I will be dismissed and forgotten by them in a matter of stoned seconds. At the same time, I'll always be in there, younguns. That's funny. I'll cease with my dummy condensation? Better to continue though. Gotta let the little bastards rest. They're goin with Dummy in the morn, catch and eat some raw mercury boys. Did I misunderstand? Did I misunderstand, today. tomorrow? Back Stabber has a lie on his tongue. Maggot man, with whore woman. Liars of no worth to Shaman, Sun, Sand, and Stars.

Ugly, empty, stupid fuckballs. Liars. I am yet to receive divorce papers from Dirt Girl. Yet drunk and drunker, encourage her to sleep with, spread dirt to, and mislead some other fuckin stupid shit bird. What a clan!!! I have moved and grooved with underworld circles, that were on the "up and up", underworld. Then I got dragged into a shit tank of liars, if not for little innocense, all would cease breathing long before now. What a filthy, dirty ugly tribe. Rather than to allow the cocksuckers to buy me a roll of shit paper, I'd defecate in their faces. Took an "innocent man" of passion, and blatantly, willingly, knowingly, plowed him asunder. Retribution they'll get. You mutthas seem to sluff it off. Not as bad as I make it out to be? All my life, I seduced tight young pussy "the eyes and the ass". No more luxuries for me. Only a matter of time, fore I snap. The mad deceit curbed my sensibility. Wrong move. Tale a wolf, from fresh kill, the wolf will lash out. Tis but natural cause and effect. I wish you that you know my level of composure. The one who knew that I was doin all in my Mohawk to maintain is dead. Onondaga is ashes. Composure is waning.

Why? Why? Must I continue with this? Tired, tired I am of all of it, yet can't seem to get enough. I must unleash every word, every thought, every sentence, laugh, tear, howl, scream, sigh, on the human fuckin race. Shut up Joel, if you had a hot young ballistic cunt, you'd hear these words at deafening decibels round about now. But alas lad, you have no overbearing cunt in your world to tell you how to act, laugh, drink, hump, dance, or ride. You lucky fucker. So you can breathe easier than your bro's that have? All I ever wanted was to please, fulfill "rise" to the occasion. Nicer you are, the meaner they'll be. Specially the hotties. They know all the wolves are lookin to please em. When they get a loyal wolf, seekin a lifetime of passion and pleasure (they can at anytime bring in other bitches) may take a decade or half of one.

Guaranteed they'll bail. Give 1 million percent, get yourself cut down. Give them 1% they "might" stick around. A women's heart is treacherous. No matter what course you take, it will

not be right, or enough, to stay the tide of emotional instabili-
ty, or dark mental treachery that is the composition of women.
Never heard of one that had their world shattered by a man.
Rather amusing? Throughout my life I have fancied their hor-
monal whims. Tried to please... ?? Fuck that shit. It's an impos-
sibility, black jack.

Now we'll roll into the "Ides of March", 21 good pages, read
thrice by Spartacus. After all, that Mohawk whore spilled his
guts on page. Stood smelling the stench of his leather, laughed,
and drank more whiskey. I'm standin, pissin, drinkin, look at the
fuckin clock. It's 4:00 a.m. I must be incensed at what I heard
and saw this evening. No fuckin wonder my head's pounding
and me ears is ringin.

Mad bell ringers and whoremasters, reprise. At this point you
might want to eat some wicked good grub. Up to you. I've
fuckin had it. That's it, none of this shit is even remotely toler-
able anymore. I have one calculated gladiatorial brother, I have
other mad sinister brothers of different stature. I have one
mad, mental, physical, spiritual, underworld, brother. Thank
you German. For you are who I speak of with such high regard.
Your skills and prowess in the arena are unsurpassed. I learn
from you, your door is my door. If by some odd circumstance,
you need the hand, heart or mind of a brother..it will rise to the
call and do all I can to honor your name.

Apologies, I am torn and cleaved in two by events of earlier
this day. I will soon not forget. Likely never, it was inevitable
that ties would be severed. I have caused a great enough rift
in family that will take long years of reparations without my
presence involved in any way, shape, or form.

I'd be catholic, drunk, whore... I'm saved as long as I ignore.
I'm buying my way to heaven. I'll mislead my babies and my
grand babies right to the pearly fuckin gates. Does anyone
want dirt for an appetizer, before an exceptionally well prepared home cooked dinner? I stay my hand, with great lack of
breathe. Conduct beyond worthy of execution. If not for the
little one... You seek to spend time and break bread with those
who shit on me and stab me in the back? Fuck all of you for
dishonoring my lutus.

You'll have to bring this word to my attention, speak with
respect. Don't be like a typical cunt and attempt to get away

with every discretion you can foment. What are ya? A natural born liar? Who is the weaker sex? Really? ... As men we make everything happen. We build, we eat, we smash foreign nations at our feet. "Men", see, cause that's what men do. Women on the other hand have an evil whip of misunderstanding. Glenn Miller, Zuit Suits, Whore Ovaries..thanks Pop... where are you right now old man??? I'm wearin your WW2 watch cap as I write. I look at your picture captured on progress. I see your direction, When I dined in the 900 year old family owned restaurant in Szombathely, Hungry I have the reproductions of what my eyes and mind recorded. Wow... Indian Ghost... you getting all this. German, I know you are.

"Alright, alright, alright" "Come on, come on, come on" The heaviest realm I've ever known, in my realm, is the inescapable fact I'm travelin, travelin, through time... laughin, absolutely... taken by the artists. Why, why, why are these power loads unleashing such energy upon me, me, me, meself. If anyone reading this can comprehend or understand yours, mine, ours, their level of ballasticness? Then you'll more than likely understand what I just wrote... After all... I'm still wearing the motherfucking Coat!!!!!!!!!!!!!!! All you can do... is all you can do!!!!! Who is real? My right shoulder aches from pen in hand, and it is a good aching! Exacting retribution would defiantly be a more gladiatorial reward. Furious feminine beauty cannot be trusted or held sacred, since the dawn of time! You listenin?

Ya'll see now that it's elevation that influences the white man's "thermometer". Humans appear to be entranced by the planetary cycles of weather? Tune in. Forget the media, the government, religious fiction... remember everything, what did I just say in the sentence prior? All you gotta do, is be yourself! No one else can do this, not even a wicked stunt double of the whiskey drinkin demon Christian sect. Indian Ghost... you fuckers stirred up a righteous pot of bullshit and lies. If at some point in mad hammerdown time, you word monger, thought eatin, mad lunatic individuals get heavy into all you know, then "rounds for the house", "kick" that motherfuckin iron horse!! Gotta get in the first three or not? Extenuating circumstances. What are ya??...a biker! Damn the level of coherence..that it takes to write like a genuine author?

It's like a Gladiator? I will gladly, with fierce sense of purpose, rise like a Warrior Shaman, Viking, Roman, Celtic, Germanic Blues man to continue on... Showing the humans that certain segments of society... might want to have ancient council, It is not easy or remotely acceptable to be an Indian Ghost, It's always been this way. When the liars, marauders, small pox, darkness, fever came what the hell were we doin? Extend your hand Warrior, Shaman, chief, women, children, extend your hand. Injustice. Black, white, yellow... where is the Red Man!?! Children of the beginning of time? It's so hard to focus on all this. All of a sudden I was engulfed by Clapton!

So back to the fuckin coat!!! Just fuckin with ya! Ink, ink, ink, get some ink. You can't rush this lunacy... yeah right dude... I am getting Jimmy Beam and Buddy Wieser just now, so relax. Or not. I have some writing to do, like a bestselling Jew. I won't mention any names, but the particular author, that I make reference to is highly recommended by mad trusted Shaman loons, so I fully endorse his mad author projection. Everyone's invited to my long house. Just be cool, I haven't riden my iron horse since, what day is it? Since 11.24.2010. CABIN MUTHERFUCKIN FEVER!!!! GET SOME, GET SOME, GET SOME, wrapped too tight on an Iroquois night. All the energy that is flowing from me, must certainly come to be? Where are these Gods you speak of?? Ones who accepts and understands the fallibility, and the infallibility, of all the energy that is exposed... shots, yager, now come on...these shots used to be a lot taller, am I mistaken!?! I like shiny things on the appendages that house my dangerous rings. Seems the "state" the "king" the "prefect" the "overlords" have deemed the ancient adornment of fully clad claws and paws an offense!!!???!!!!

If I could just "write" constantly... may my thoughts flow freely till I'm empty! Lets toe the line. I can give you my word as an "American Madman", that I will not forsake my origin. Tough claim in the fast lane of what has been written of for ions and centuries.

I talked to Ma excitedly 2 days back. She embarrassingly asked of me if my book contained vulgarity? "Absolutely!" I proclaimed. My Roman Catholic Lay Minister mom, will likely never get past her third son's mad writings, it's a given. That's ok. Some folks ain't cut out for things that they ain't cut out for hahahahaha.

Listen "German". This project must be taken to the edge of human reason, Come on, come on, come on, wacky cacky sings. Lost the Coozy again. Yager??? Only 3 shots of darkness straight up! Fuck the yuppie "yager bombs." What the fuck got me so hemorrhaged, so hammered that the ever elusive Banditos Coozy once again slipped through my... ...grasp. It's bound to turn up, mad great gift from Choctaw, Shaman, Warrior! The energy of life only goes unnoticed by unreal. Those who genuinely exude reality are duly noted by the real. What happened to the Coozy again? You are suppose to keep some sort of tabs on these matters, fuckball.

Why did I just take all that out? Blue maybe? That's the way it has to be, blues maybe?... How much do you think you can put across? Come on, it's fuckin pissin down rain. Let's wait for a couple more blastin throat gulps of fire water. By then it ought to be sky opened up plenty pissin down hard November rain and we'll fire the horses and ride into a frozen wet hurricane. They must be goin to see a valued brother. The romancers can party and dance.

Put, put, put, this, that, and the other thing in your fuckin book, shitbird. Film makers, painters, singers, musicians, writers, dancers, killers, surfers, laughers, mad bikers, this must continue to unfold. The unique culture of our unraveling and gathering.

Listen man, or not... do yourselves a favor and don't. Small black insects race feverishly on the surface of my kitchen table, what fuckin time is it? 12:50 a.m. I'll drink more Satanic devil's urine tasty beverages ha ha ha ha ha ha fuck off Spartacus you arrogant prick tough guy, fucking scum AUTHOR'S NOTE: "Just speakin my mind.: It's constitutional don't you European marauders know?

Hey... you need any smallpox? Let's cut your hair and stop your singing and dancing in the name of our genocide God and the fucking whore fucking republic... PISS OFF YOU FUCKING PARASITES. If someone told you that it was absolutely mandatory that you changed your name, stop speaking your tongue, cut off your hair, no longer wear your comfortable custom clothes, no singin, no dancing, shut down your trading network, your sun and wind and moon and stars. All the gifts that you openly, freely gave were piss in the wind? Who would not want to exact payment as a Warrior? The place and purpose of a Shaman can only go so far in the corrupt white dominated garbage political system that has overrun us.

If freedom drives your carnal soul, then act heavy, aggressive. Easy to write about... lash out! Take all of our land back from lies and tyranny. Read and believe these writings. Rise up Indian Ghosts, This will happen, it must. It will. Too many moons, under the sun to pass the interchange of dark beautiful truth up without some tough fuckin Warrior standin up!!!

Too bad I ain't 27. I can't even believe the loss of the Coozy! What is this? A new era? Somehow or another I must refuse to stop. Stop what?? Hot, heart shaped girl butt? Who can resist a tight cherry, ass round, bottom wicked, pretty, big eyed, lashes, hips, full sensual lips, cock sucking, jaw line, bad selfish attitude, blonde, brunette, red head? Is that a shallow male statement? Every extremely good lookin, sex kitten, that I have encountered is naught more than a destroyer of men. Lost my banditos Coozy? Better focus and find... track down.

Them fuckin cats are ballistic man. Gonzo book, book in Gonzo, what do ya say? What do ya write? Got any peyote? How about mashin the wind with "Ape Hangers" Fight, relax, listen, drink. Gotta luv eating hot, tight, young pretty pink. So provocative, promise you everything. Love eyes, silk thighs, real sighs.

Just givin you what you wanna hear, trapped, bum bullshit steer. They sure are pretty though, Tell you all you wanna hear, Right outta the gate. I don't want an internet relationship. I want maximum carnal. How, how, how can this scenario play out? My life has been shattered. Time for me to do some life shatterin of me own. Cristin says "That good Karma is headin my way?" and "what time is it now?" It's 2:00 a.m. Why am I alone? Betrayal. You want everything under the sun. Have at it. Respect me. Give me passion. Give me understanding. Be my friend, my lover, my companion. What the fuck is so tough about that request... girl???

2.17.2011 10:30 a.m. So I just choked and Stitch almost puked on a thick brutal Cactus asscloud. Anyway, I called Jesus and he found "no Coozy" upon cleaning the kitchen before work. I vaguely remember placing my Coozied Brew on the top of the Buick when leaving the Shaman convention while pissing. Sure enough, Stitch came over to help me chop pool table size ice blocks outta my way of walking and I told him what happened so we drove towards Jesus and Roxies longhouse until the Coozy was sighted, waiting for me in the slush on the side of the road... not so elusive are ya Coozy? Nice and so it begins...

"Quest for knowledge. Who am I a primitive? (Flip open napkin) Tough draggin it out o your brain 2,3,4,5 days later, What are you? Nuts? "Mad Mad Mad" I say. Where you headed now?

POST SCRIPT

The following page is "strictly" the lunacy. "The Incoherent Ramblings of an American Madman©" are open to further interpretation. I threw a hook in at the end. I figured that any of you folks that read this far, may, or may not have seen the twisted Shaman hook fucking coming at you right from page one? Thank you, good night, Gonzo.

"Yeah , I finished this on my fucking birthday! So what!?!

Everyone on this planet will know who I am. Audacious? When this one goes mad global, I'm figuring the next could be filmed by some mad pro like Tarantino, Rodriquez, maybe "the Dude" or "Alec". One never can tell who will catch creativity. Probably like a ghost, Jimbo, "an Indian Ghost".

Enlighten little kids and intrigue your elders for they are your past and your future. What's left of any of it any fucking way? So, somewhere on the frontier a Lakota Sioux drum circle did a tribute to Stevie Ray Vaughn and the sacred musicians from the dawn of time sang and danced. The ghosts knew that all music sprang from them. The first people. The Indian Ghosts.

Tough to shut it down sometimes. It's good for the writer to write, drink, laugh, and dance all night. Twist the throttle. Kick start the mad horse and roll into the last, next text. I didn't hump a tight young hard belly on my 48th this time around. Back to "so fucking what".

Can I write anything relevant? Anything at all?

Special thanks to Jamie Sutor, R.I.P. and Dave Ferguson,

FUCK EVERYTHING!

Don't get me started, here I go, get some of this... Fuck wall street, fuck the internet, fuck politicians, fuck religion, fuck the pope, fuck China, fuck television, fuck the President, fuck advertising, fuck cocaine, fuck charity, fuck stupidity, fuck longevity, fuck oil, fuck fast food, fuck war, fuck propaganda, fuck credit cards, fuck bottled water, fuck voting, fuck cell phones, fuck automobiles, fuck prisons, fuck banks, fuck corporate America, fuck rap, fuck the KKK, fuck the NAACP, fuck congress, fuck republicans, fuck democrats, fuck Catholics, fuck protestants, fuck Baptists, fuck Lutherans, fuck Muslims, fuck Conservatives, fuck Liberals, fuck mimes, fuck clowns, fuck terrorists, fuck the fda, fuck DEA, fuck FBI, fuck ATF, fuck plastic, fuck Israel, fuck Palestine, fuck whites, fuck blacks, fuck Jews, fuck Mexicans, fuck poodles, fuck wallabies, fuck Japanese, fuck whales, fuck cities, fuck bombs, fuck mines, fuck unicycles, fuck sitcoms, fuck ignorance, fuck hate, fuck love, fuck trust, fuck welfare, fuck the system, fuck Christianity, fuck liars, fuck rapists, fuck murderers, fuck child molesters, fuck rabbis, fuck priests, fuck nuns, fuck special interest groups, fuck the rich, fuck Nazis, fuck Hindus, fuck rednecks, fuck investors, fuck commerce, fuck soccer, fuck soccer fans, fuck evolution, fuck creation, fuck capitalism, fuck white bread, fuck wall street again, fuck growth hormones, fuck true TV, fuck Oprah, fuck gay rights, fuck Anarchy, fuck sports, fuck ex-wives, fuck kindness, fuck sympathy, fuck pills, fuck cancer, fuck the Vatican, fuck my birthday, fuck dirt, fuck fisherman, fuck snow shovels, fuck soccer moms, fuck snow blowers and those that use them, and fuck all you mother fuckers that bought my book... to be continued... but last but not least, fuck me and fuck my book.

Nutshell

Chapter 13

Well, I must say that was a pretty show. Took quite a few moons to watch and I was only able to put a fleeting glimpse to paper. There's so much more to be done, written, seen and heard. Just a taste, an appetizer of what's to come.

So many times in this life we're faced with the end, but really, is it the end? Is there actually such a concept? I've come to the conclusion that there is no end, not even in death. It's merely a change in ones circumstances, that's all it is. I've found in my life, many times I thought it was the end of the line, desperate and devastated, lost of family, health, wealth, love... thought I couldn't go on... crazy old adage "time heals all wounds" wounds get deeper, scar tissue heavier, more jaded but at the same time you become stronger/

I find I have gained more as a human being with each episode of loss? Strange, but true. I've had some great people in my corner, though I thought I might not want to listen to them at the time, but they were expressing to me don't "quit." Especially my mom, she always said "be strong, you are strong like your father, you gotta keep going, I know there is more in my son than this."

My old man said "Life's what you make it, you got yourself into this, you are the only one that's going to get you out it." Even if there's a lot of others who have contributed, you owe it to yourself to continue on. The human condition, people get lost, since the dawn of time but there are so many ways to find oneself again. Speaking from vast experience here.

I guess it all boils down to respect. A huge word. One we all need to know more deeply. Respect for self and everyone else who is worthy, who show themselves worthy of it. Don't follow blindly though. Lead with respect. Listen and learn for the elders. Much wisdom will be gained from mutual respect. Even if life is beating you to a proverbial pulp, it's not necessarily the end.

Don't quit, don't lie down, do not go quietly. Maintain your dignity. Whatever straits you find yourself in... press on. Return to the elements. Nature will always be big medicine. Pat attention to the ancient Native American culture.

Experience as much in life as you possibly can. Grab the bull by the horns and get out there and see the world. It takes many lifetimes to finish school. Continue on in the quest for knowledge. Do whatever you can to practice love and respect in your life and we can pull through with our honor intact.

If we don't want to be kicked around in this life, then let your actions prove worthy. Don't be kickin people around. Give away a lot of love. Life is loaded up with good and bad. Choose wisely, on one's own level, a course that will be a benefit to self and all you cross paths with on life's journey.

Respect, it comes back around. Exercise it in all things. Moderation or excess? Drugs and alcohol or sobriety? Whatever it is we do, we should all have self respect. Whenever we can lets help each other out. Continue to learn ways of inner peace and go out of the way to teach them and pass them along. Life and death should be equally celebrated. Keep your eyes and ears open. Perseverance. If it can be written, it can be done. The German and I thought this would be something really tasty to chew on after plowing through the "ramblings." Whose pay-in attention? "Take from this what personally benefits you or tickles your ears." I would highly recommend that everyone read "Shaman's Circle" poems by Nancy Wood and paintings by Frank Howell. Double day book.

Thank you for participating.

Spartacus

Me, Otis (R.I.P.), and Cactus, 2006

The author's writings at his kitchen table, Winter 2011"

Fin

"Burn this Book at Will"

CPSIA information can be obtained at www.ICGtesting.com
Printed in the USA
BVOW04s1045030214

343603BV00001B/5/P